A sting in the tale

A sting in the tale

Roy Clements

Inter-Varsity Press

INTER-VARSITY PRESS
38 De Montfort Street, Leicester LE1 7GP, England

Unless otherwise stated, quotations from the Bible are taken
from the Holy Bible: New International Version. Copyright
© 1973, 1978, 1984 International Bible Society. Published
in Great Britain by Hodder and Stoughton Ltd.

First published 1995
Reprinted 1996, 1997

British Library Cataloguing in Publication Data
A catalogue record for this book is available from the British
Library.

ISBN 0–85110–881–4

Set in Linotype Palatino

Typeset in Great Britain by Parker Typesetting Service,
Leicester

Printed and bound in Great Britain by
Cox & Wyman Ltd, Reading, Berkshire

Inter-Varsity Press is the book-publishing division of the
Universities and Colleges Christian Fellowship (formerly the
Inter-Varsity Fellowship), a student movement linking
Christian Unions in universities and colleges throughout the
United Kingdom and the Republic of Ireland, and a member
movement of the International Fellowship of Evangelical
Students. For information about local and national activities
write to UCCF, 38 De Montfort Street, Leicester LE1 7GP.

Contents

Introduction

Everyone loves a story. Stories are universal and timeless. They can bridge the gap between people of different ages, social backgrounds and cultures. They don't just inform the mind, they engage the heart. And though they can be immensely entertaining, stories can also sometimes be very profound too.

Jesus loved to tell stories, or 'parables', as he called them. This book examines several of the most famous which are preserved for us in the gospel of Luke. Maybe a word or two about parables generally will be helpful before we begin to study some particular examples.

Jesus' parables fall into two broad categories. Some are simply extended similes. The kingdom of God is like a pearl of great value (Matthew 13:45–46) or a net cast in the sea (Matthew 13:47). Such parables are coded visual aids. They illustrate a particular spiritual truth that Jesus is trying to get across, but in a deliberately cryptic fashion. There's another sort of parable, though, in which Luke is particularly interested. This kind goes further than simply being an extended simile. It's much closer to being an allegorical story. In these 'parable tales' Jesus is not merely seeking to tantalize or educate his hearers; he's wanting to challenge them at a fundamental level. On the surface, such stories seem innocuous; charming little narratives full of familiar images that easily capture your attention. In reality they're a kind of Stealth bomber, specially designed to evade our psychological defences, insinuating themselves inside our mind in spite of every barricade we may seek to erect, and then dropping a highly explosive charge targeted at the most vulnerable point in our spiritual complacency.

One feature that is often characteristic of these story parables is that they have a sting in the tail; a punch-line that creeps up on you and then kicks you in the stomach when you're not expecting it. In some respects, that makes these parables peculiarly difficult to re-tell today. Some of them have become so well known that they're part of our cultural furniture, and as a result, have lost much of their original novelty value. The good Samaritan and the prodigal son, for instance, are so familiar that their punch-lines no longer convey the same shock. We're waiting for it; it doesn't take us by surprise. Worse still, perhaps, even the lack of surprise doesn't surprise us.

With a little bit of imagination, however, it is not impossible to recapture the original impact of these stories. It means that we have to project ourselves back into being one of Jesus' original audience. Then at least in measure we can rediscover just how subversive and radical these parables of his really were. That at any rate is our aim in this book. We are going to try to find 'the sting in the tale', if you'll forgive the pun. If we succeed – if Jesus' Stealth bombers find their target in us – then beware! We shall not be left the same after their attack. Each one carries a one-megaton charge guaranteed to blow your mind!

Originally these eight chapters were all sermons preached in various contexts. Some were given to the Keswick Convention, and I am grateful for permission to reproduce that material here. The remainder were delivered at Eden Chapel, Cambridge, in the course of normal Sunday services. Thanks are due to the staff of IVP who have performed the hard work of transcribing those addresses from tape recordings. In both cases the sermon text has been only lightly edited and the reader will often catch the flavour of oral style as a result. Maybe that is appropriate, for Jesus' parables were all originally spoken to a live audience, too.

Roy Clements

1

The seed of change

Luke 8:1–15

After this, Jesus travelled about from one town and village to another, proclaiming the good news of the kingdom of God. The Twelve were with him, ²*and also some women who had been cured of evil spirits and diseases: Mary (called Magdalene) from whom seven demons had come out;* ³*Joanna the wife of Chuza, the manager of Herod's household; Susanna; and many others. These women were helping to support them out of their own means.*

⁴*While a large crowd was gathering and people were coming to Jesus from town after town, he told this parable:* ⁵*'A farmer went out to sow his seed. As he was scattering the seed, some fell along the path; it was trampled on, and the birds of the air ate it up.* ⁶*Some fell on rock, and when it came up, the plants withered because they had no moisture.* ⁷*Other seed fell among thorns, which grew up with it and choked the plants.* ⁸*Still other seed fell on good soil. It came up and yielded a crop, a hundred times more than was sown.'*

When he said this, he called out, 'He who has ears to hear, let him hear.'

⁹*His disciples asked him what this parable meant.* ¹⁰*He said, 'The knowledge of the secrets of the kingdom of God has been given to you, but to others I speak in parables, so that,*

> *"though seeing, they may not see;*
> *though hearing, they may not understand."*

¹¹*'This is the meaning of the parable: The seed is the word of God.* ¹²*Those along the path are the ones who hear, and then the devil comes and takes away the word from their hearts, so that they may not believe and be saved.* ¹³*Those on the rock are the*

ones who receive the word with joy when they hear it, but they have no root. They believe for a while, but in the time of testing they fall away. [14]The seed that fell among thorns stands for those who hear, but as they go on their way they are choked by life's worries, riches and pleasures, and they do not mature. [15]But the seed on good soil stands for those with a noble and good heart, who hear the word, retain it, and by persevering produce a crop.'

They were coming from all directions, like fans converging on a football ground. They came alone, they came in groups. Husbands brought their wives, mothers brought their children, youths brought their mates. Some seemed to have brought their whole town with them. They came because they were sick and handicapped and thought he might heal them. They came because they were poor and oppressed and thought he might deliver them. They came because they were bored and curious and thought he might amuse them. They came . . . well, some of them would have had a hard job explaining why exactly they had come, except that everybody else was coming. But with whatever company and with whatever motivation they came, there was one word on Jesus' lips which intrigued and excited them all: 'kingdom'.

'The kingdom of God has come.' That's what they said he was preaching. For the rural masses of Galilee those words were like sparks on dry tinder.

Every society has its dream of a better world: the classless society, the American dream, Utopia; and first-century Jews were no exception. Down through the latter years of the Old Testament period, as inspired prophets had wrestled with their national experience of tyranny and oppression, a dream of a coming kingdom gained sharper and sharper focus in their minds. It became clear that it would take an extraordinary intervention on God's part to transform this present evil world into the sort of world where God's people would really feel at home. A decisive victory over the power of evil would have to be won, a victory no ordinary human being could achieve.

So they looked forward to the arrival of a supernatural deliverer, one who would be anointed like the mighty heroes of the past: a new David, but greater even than David was. They waited, in a word, for the Messiah. 'Don't worry,' said the prophets, 'things are pretty bad for us Jews in this present evil age. But soon the Messiah will step out of the wings of history. And then, at long last, the kingdom of God will begin.'

Can you imagine the shock, the tremor of hope that must have gone through the population of Galilee when Jesus, a young carpenter from Nazareth, started to wander around their towns and villages saying it had happened? 'The kingdom of God has come. Repent and believe the good news,' he said.

No doubt initially many were sceptical. They were not unfamiliar with lunatics who indulged their megalomaniac fantasies by pretensions to be the Messiah. But this man did not just make messianic claims. He cast out demons. He healed the sick. And he taught; oh, how he taught! There was a charisma about him that had not been seen in Israel since the days of the greatest prophets half a millennium before. There was even a rumour that he was Elijah or Jeremiah risen from the dead. That was the measure of the astonishing impact he had made.

Had he wanted to exploit the opportunity, he could have set in motion a bandwagon of religious revival and political revolution that the authorities in Jerusalem and perhaps even in Rome would have been unable to stop. That word 'kingdom' resonated with all the Galilean masses' most glorious dreams, fired their most fanatical zeal and inspired their most passionate commitment. All he had to do when confronted by this vast multitude was to work a miracle or two and deliver a suitably firebrand speech; the whole of the Galilean countryside would have erupted in volcanic enthusiasm for his messiahship.

But the extraordinary thing is, he didn't. Instead, he told them a story. Can you imagine it, this great crowd coming to him from town after town, full of expectancy, hanging on his every word, longing to be moved with emotive oratory and impressed by supernatural power – and he sits down and tells them a story! A bizarre, perplexing riddle of a story at that: a 'parable', he calls it.

Even his closest friends were utterly bewildered by his behaviour. 'What on earth are you doing, Jesus?' they asked him. 'What is this parable business all about?' That's when he explained it to them.

> The knowledge of the secrets of the kingdom of God has been given to you, but to others I speak in parables, so that,
>
> > 'though seeing, they may not see;
> > though hearing, they may not understand.'
> >
> > (Luke 8:10).

Unpopular and controversial words. They contradict the popular view of parables as moralizing stories told in picturesque imagery to aid the understanding of simple, unsophisticated rural people. On the contrary, Jesus says he speaks in parables not to make it *easier* for people to understand, but to make it *harder*. 'Though seeing, they may not see; though hearing, they may not understand.'

Whatever you make of that, it's quite clear that Jesus was not as impressed by these crowds, streaming out of all Galilee to see him, as we might have been if we'd been there. He was not at all convinced that they were really on his wavelength. He'd grown up among them, you see. He knew perfectly well what their ideas of the kingdom of God were, and they were as different from his own ideas as chalk from cheese. The last thing he wanted to do was to foster their mistaken notions by courting popularity with them. He hints, in fact, that he feels rather as the prophet Isaiah did, when he was told to preach to a people whose hearts would be irredeemably hardened against his words. In Isaiah's day it seems that Israel had become so infatuated by pagan idols that they could neither see nor hear that God had judicially abandoned them to spiritual blindness and deafness themselves.

It's that divine decree from Isaiah 6:9 which Jesus is quoting when he speaks in verse 10 of listeners who cannot understand. The Galilean masses, according to Jesus, are in a similar spiritual state to the Jews of Isaiah's Jerusalem. They are incapable of comprehending the new revelation of the kingdom of God which he had brought because their minds are prejudicially closed against it. Some commentators go so far as to conclude from verse 10 that Jesus deliberately adopted a strategy of conceal-ment, of hiding his true opinions from the masses. They suggest that he was so disillusioned with the Jewish people and convinced that like Isaiah's Jerusalem they would reject him in the end, that he deliberately camouflaged his message to confirm them in their condemned state of unbelief.

It's an arguable theory, but I think it somewhat overstates the case. After all, if Jesus wanted to conceal his message from the crowds altogether, why preach at all? And what are we to make of the impassioned exhortation, 'He who has ears to hear, let him hear'? That certainly sounds as if he desires an intelligent response to his words.

I think it's closer to the truth to interpret Jesus as saying in verse 10 that he uses parables as a kind of filter. Among the thousands who come out to see him for all the wrong reasons, he believes there are some who are genuinely open to the truth. A tiny minority, maybe, amid that vast, spiritually deaf multitude; but though few, they did have ears to hear. His parables were a filter that identified those true disciples. Those who came to Jesus looking for just a political leader, a nationalist revolutionary or a spell-binding miracle-worker went away disillusioned. They found, to their disappointment, just a teller of stories. But those who were drawn to him by some deeper magnetism stayed. In their hearts God's Spirit was working. They were being inwardly called to follow him. Though they were perplexed at first, just like all the others, they were also intrigued, longing to understand what he was really getting at, sensing that somewhere buried in the tantalizing obscurity of his parables lay the clue to that kingdom of God for which their hearts longed. 'To you,' he says to them, 'the knowledge of the secrets of the kingdom of God has been given.' This is in fact a fundamental characteristic of all Jesus' ministry. You don't get to grips with his message from the safe distance of a detached curiosity. Spiritual illumination is the privilege of those who are personally committed to him, and share the intimacy of a personal relationship with him. Unlike so many orators, Jesus' head was never turned by the flattery of the crowds. He wasn't fooled by the illusion of success that big numbers conjure up. The 'megachurch' mentality with its consumer-oriented 'gospel according to market research' held no appeal for him. He saw through it. He was perfectly content to invest himself in just the twelve men and the handful of women whom Luke names for us. Provided they were real learners, real disciples, he was prepared to give the whole of himself to such a tiny band.

Significantly, the interpretation of the parables that Jesus goes on to unfold elucidates this sifting process further. Behind the pastoral imagery of the sower and the seed is the solemn and serious truth that only some who hear his words are ultimately blessed by him. Tragically, many are evangelized, and yet not saved. Though the initial response may look promising, the path of discipleship proves too demanding.

Before we look at that interpretation in detail, it is

worth noting that the simple fact that Jesus does interpret his parables in this fashion explodes two common contemporary theories about parables. Some recent New Testament commentators have argued that parables should not be interpreted at all, but simply retold in contemporary dress. A parable, they argue, is a rhetorical device that's designed to make an immediate impact on a live audience, so to interpret a parable is a bit like explaining a joke. The punch-line is bound to get lost in the very attempt to do so.

There is a profound element of truth in that view. Parables are deliberately mysterious and elusive. There is an air of paradox and surprise which is intended to subvert the presuppositions of the listener. By drawing us into his story Jesus disarms our psychological defences so that unwelcome and unpalatable truths can strike home to our hearts like a missile seeking its target. And in consequence it is undoubtedly difficult to preach the parables in a way that recovers that original dramatic impact. Nevertheless, Jesus clearly believed neither that it was impossible to explain parables, nor that their point was irretrievably lost in the process of trying to do so; because here he interprets a parable himself.

A second thesis commonly defended by scholars today, and also contradicted by Jesus' example here, is that parables are sermon illustrations designed to make a single point, and therefore should never be treated as allegories. Once again, there's an important element of truth in this. Medieval scholars sometimes allowed their imaginations to run riot in seeking hidden allegorical meanings within parables.

For example, if you study the conclusion of this parable in the gospels of Matthew and Mark, you'll find it ends slightly differently. The seed on the good ground yields varying quantities of harvest: some a hundred-fold, as here in Luke's account, but also some sixty-fold and some thirty-fold. Luke has abbreviated the story slightly in this respect. Medieval commentators eagerly seized upon the longer ending and engaged in all kinds of speculative ideas about its significance. One popular theory was that the hundred-fold yield represented martyrs who had given their lives for Christ; the sixty-fold yield represented monks who had taken a vow of celibacy; and the thirty-fold yield? 'Well,' it was argued, 'obviously the thirty-fold yield represents those whose diminutive contribution to the kingdom of God is simply that of being an obedient wife!'

Clearly such a reading of Jesus' picture language is illegitimate. There's no reason at all for believing that he intends to make any comment about martyrs, monks or obedient wives in the parable of the sower. Much of the detail in his parables in fact has no hidden, secondary meaning at all, but is there simply to add colour to the story.

It will not do, however, to insist that parables have only a single lesson to teach. For Jesus' own interpretation of this parable has decidedly allegorical features. The sower, the seed, the stony ground and the weeds all stand for different things. So it's clearly a mistake to draw too sharp a line between parable and allegory, or to place some arbitrary limit on how much teaching content a parable may be intended to convey.

In fact, I want to suggest to you that there are at least three vital lessons which Jesus is trying to communicate in this parable.

1. How the kingdom of God progresses

This is the meaning of the parable: The seed is the word of God (Luke 8:11).

We began with Jesus' gripping announcement of the kingdom of God. The powers of evil are fleeing before his face. Demons are being exorcised. Cripples are being healed. The signs of his messianic mission to transform the world are clearly apparent. But how is the world to be changed? That's the inevitable question: how is the kingdom to be brought in? What strategy will Jesus employ to precipitate this decisive transformation in world history? Will he raise up an angelic army and march on Jerusalem or Rome? Will he call down supernatural fire from heaven to consume the wicked? What means does he intend to use to bring in the kingdom of God? This was in fact a great source of debate among Jews in his day. And it is the answer to that very question to which he refers when he speaks of the 'secrets of the kingdom of God'. He claims to bring privileged information on this vital point from the highest possible intelligence source in the universe, from heaven itself. And the clue to that secret strategy, for those who are able to penetrate the parable in which it is encoded, lies in the cipher of the seed.

Putting the evidence of all his parables and teaching together, it is clear that Jesus anticipated that the kingdom of God would come in a way hitherto unforeseen by the Jewish people. It would arrive in three phases, rather than in a single apocalyptic crisis. First, there would be a time of *planting* as the Messiah arrived, incognito and disguised, to sow the seed of the kingdom in the hearts of a few chosen disciples. Then there would be a period of *growth* as that seed, multiplied through their testimony, fertilized many other lives until eventually the spores of the kingdom had become distributed throughout the world. And finally there would be a time of *reaping* when the Messiah would return, this time amid universal public acclamation, to harvest the fruit which the seed he had sown had produced, and so bring in the full manifestation of the kingdom of which the prophets had spoken.

So the answer to that vital question, 'How is the kingdom of God to arrive?' lies in the metaphor of the seed. And what is that seed, this vital instrument by which the new world of the kingdom is sown in the very midst of the old world? Here in his first parable Jesus leaves his disciples in no doubt on that point. 'The seed', he says, 'is the word.' The preaching of the gospel will be the seminal agent of change. It will germinate God's cosmic revolution. It brings in the kingdom. 'The seed is the word of God.'

It's hard to overestimate the importance of that single brief sentence. Sadly, the church through the centuries has not always believed it. Again and again, other things have usurped the prime place the Word ought to have on the Christian agenda. Once, for instance, the church revered bread and wine more than the Bible; the altar instead of the pulpit stood at the centre not only of her architecture but also of her theology.

There are still those who even today would take us back to such sacramentalist superstition if they could. But in our generation the threat to the primacy of the Word has usually come from other directions: social action, for instance. In recent years many Christians have become much more politically involved. For too long, Christians have treated the political arena as a no-go area, as if Jesus were Lord of everywhere else except there. Not so. Christians have a responsibility to be the salt of the earth in Council offices and in parliamentary debates, just as much as through evangelistic crusades or overseas missions.

Nevertheless, there is a danger of over-compensating for our previous neglect of social issues. People can lose touch with Jesus' priorities. The pendulum can swing to the opposite extreme. God's new society is not brought in by Act of Parliament, still less by machine gun. It is brought in through the Word.

Jesus was familiar enough with the revolutionary politics of his own day. Many of the zealot freedom fighters came from his home area of Galilee. But their tactics were not for him. It was the wrong seed, and he knew it. The seed is the Word. A Word which, when you hear it on the lips of Jesus and his disciples, does not concern itself directly with social and economic structures; a Word which offers no utopian strategy for the immediate overturn of institutional evil; a Word, rather, which is about personal repentance, personal forgiveness, personal faith and personal discipleship. It is a Word which, as we observe in this very parable, is targeted not on the politicized masses but on the hearts of responsive individuals. Notice the third person singular in Jesus' invitation: 'He who has ears to hear, let him hear' (Luke 8:8).

Superficially, no doubt, this seems a most unpromising strategy. How can we possibly bring about the dramatic transformation to which the prophets referred when they spoke of the kingdom of God merely by a 'Word'? But Jesus was convinced of it. That's why he eschewed the political path and chose instead to be a preacher and a teacher. That Word, as we shall see in our next parable, demands social action of a most practical and sacrificial kind. Jesus was certainly not unconcerned about political structures and economic injustice. But he insists that it is the Word that must come first. By his own public ministry he modelled his conviction that 'the seed is the Word of God'.

2. Inevitable failure and disappointment

Some fell on rock (Luke 8:6).

Look carefully at how Jesus tells the story. He describes, you notice, one homogeneous sowing and four different soils. If a modern expert in the science of advertising were to tell the parable, it might well be the other way round. He would speak of one homogeneous soil and four different sowers. 'The first sower sowed the seed this way, but it didn't work; the second sower used a different tactic, but that was no good either; the third tried yet another method, but still had no success; and then finally along came the sower who had done his market research and perfected his advertising technique, and so he got a harvest. Well done, sower!'

'No!' says Jesus. That's not the way it is. The success or failure of the seed of the Word does not seem to depend on the sower's technique at all. On the contrary, the seed is sown in what seems like an artless, almost wasteful way that demands no skill at all. It's just 'scattered'. For it is not the function of the sower to change one soil into another. It is rather, says Jesus, the function of the seed to highlight the intrinsic fertility or infertility of the soil. It is the quality of the soil, not the expertise of the sower, that determines the harvest.

Of course, we don't like that. It robs us of our best excuse for our rejection of the gospel, namely that the preacher was no good. It is the soil that makes the difference. Spiritual fertility does not lie in the gift of the teacher. But Jesus insists that this is the way it is. Spiritual fertility does not lie in the gift of the evangelist. And for that reason he must anticipate three categories of disappointment.

a. Those along the path

> . . . the ones who hear, and then the devil comes and takes away the word from their hearts . . . (Luke 8:12).

Jesus is candid here about the prolific waste of effort which sharing the good news of God's kingdom will often seem to be. As he speaks, he's looking out at that vast crowd, who are streaming to hear him. Many would be tempted, I'm sure, to label these casual adherents as 'converts'. After all, the mere fact that they were coming to Jesus from their homes surely indicates some kind of spiritual response, doesn't it? But Jesus is not so easily convinced. 'No,' he says, 'this is a very mixed multitude I see. Some of these people who have come out to hear me are quite obviously hardened against my Word.' That hardening may come from intellectual pride: 'He doesn't seriously expect me to believe that, does he?' Or from moral obstinacy: 'There's no way I'm going to stop doing that, just because he says so.' Or from self-righteousness: 'Me, a sinner? How dare he!' Or it may be simply the hardening of bored indifference: 'Guess this just isn't my scene. I'm into yoga, you see.'

Though they had come to hear his Word, it bounced off them like water off a duck's back. Their hearts were coated in spiritual Teflon, so nothing stuck. Perhaps they thought they were being clever, sophisticated, not taken in by all that 'kingdom of God' nonsense. But notice the one whom Jesus identifies as silently and secretly campaigning behind this defiant, cynical attitude. 'The devil comes and takes away the Word so they can't believe and be saved,' he says.

Jesus is convinced that a personal force of evil is at work seeking to discredit the Word, and to distract minds from giving attention to it. Every evangelist encounters his demonic opposition. Perhaps he's at work among readers of this book too?

b. Those on the rock

> . . . the ones who receive the word with joy when
> they hear it, but they have no root . . . (Luke 8:13).

Others in the crowd represent only a superficial decision, an initial enthusiasm that doesn't last. Their response to the Word is pure emotion, the kind of animal excitement that you get from being part of a big crowd, or the kind of warm fuzzies that you get from watching a sentimental movie. They 'receive the word with joy', says Jesus, but then circumstances change, the adrenalin subsides, the intoxication of the moment fades. Perhaps they begin to feel cheated. 'They told me Christianity made you feel happy. Well, I don't! They told me

Christianity would give me friends. Well, I haven't got any! It must have been just an adolescent phase I went through, just a flash in the pan. I'm not going to be a Christian any longer.'

'They have no root. They believe for a while, but in the time of testing they apostatize,' says Jesus. Who hasn't observed this? The spiritual five-minute wonders. For a while they're wonderful Christians. They go through all the baptismal or confirmation classes. They get involved in everything. But six months later they're nowhere to be seen.

c. Those among thorns

> . . . those who hear, but as they go on their way they are choked . . . and they do not mature . . . (Luke 8:14).

There are still others who turn out to be distracted disciples. Again, there's an enthusiastic initial response. But unlike the case of the superficial decision, these people do not seem to renege on their commitment to Jesus altogether. They retain some kind of Christian identity. They don't 'fall away' in that sense. But as time goes on, Christ becomes less and less significant in their lives. The couchgrass of rival interests clogs their energies. The bindweed of materialism and worldliness saps all those early hopes of spirituality.

In youth, perhaps, it is educational goals, sporting achievement or sexual attraction that's responsible for this diversion of interest. In mid-life it's financial stress, family responsibilities, or career ambition. In old age it's preoccupation with health, the garden or the grand-children. Whatever stage in life we're at, there are dozens of such distractions. 'As they go on their way,' says Jesus, 'they are choked by life's worries, riches and pleasures.' And the result is that 'they do not mature'. They're in a state of arrested spiritual development.

They call themselves Christian, but it's become just a church-going habit, not a vital, personal faith.

Make no mistake about it, telling the good news of God's kingdom is full of discouragement. Many people will hear and never return. Others will rush to make a decision for Christ, only to disappear. Still others will sit in the pew week after week like passengers on a train, but never display anything more than a nominal commitment.

In all this scene of disappointment there is, however, one comfort for the evangelist.

3. Enduring evidence

> *Still other seed fell on good soil. It came up and yielded a crop, a hundred times more than was sown* (Luke 8:8).

The seed of the Word is the only way to increase the kingdom. And increase it will. In spite of frustrating losses and wasted efforts, Jesus assures us that the farmer will have a splendid crop at the end of the day. For there are those who 'with a noble and good heart . . . hear the word, retain it, and by persevering produce a crop' (Luke 8:15).

Commentators disagree about how many of these four soils may represent hope of salvation. All agree that the seed sown along the path certainly does not. The text itself excludes such a possibility. 'They cannot believe and be saved,' says Jesus of those hardened hearts.

But there are many who would like to argue that the other three soils, though differing in the degree of spirituality which they represent, all nevertheless represent a saving response to the gospel. 'After all,' they say, 'the seed sown among the stones and among the weeds still germinates, doesn't it? The Word is received. A decision for Christ is made. The path of discipleship is at least begun. Such responsive individuals are surely assured of eternal life. Even if their lack of sustained commitment and spiritual growth forfeits some heavenly rewards, it can't forfeit heaven itself.'

I am unconvinced by that optimistic viewpoint. What, I ask myself, about Jesus' searching words in the Sermon on the Mount about those nominal disciples who had made a verbal profession? 'Not everyone who says to me, "Lord, Lord," will enter the kingdom of heaven, but only he who does the will of my Father who is in heaven. Many will say to me on that day, "Lord, Lord . . ." [and] I will tell them plainly, "I never knew you. Away from me . . .!"' (Matthew 7:21–23). Or what about that solemn picture of the vine he gives us in the gospel of John? 'The branch which does not bear fruit', he says, 'is cut off, and thrown into the fire' (see John 15:6). What about the solemn warning to apostates in the letter to the Hebrews? 'Land that produces thorns and thistles is worthless,' says the writer. 'In the end it will be burned' (Hebrews 6:8). What about the frightening admonition of the risen Christ to those half-hearted so-called believers in the church at Laodicea? 'Because you are lukewarm . . . I am about to spit you out of my mouth' (Revelation 3:16).

The implication of this parable is that for Jesus the only adequate response to the Word is one that issues in an enduring spiritual productivity. Nothing less would do. John F. MacArthur put it very well in *The Gospel According to Jesus*:

> Fruit-bearing is the whole point of agriculture.
> In the harvest weedy soil offers no more hope
> than does the hard road or the shallow ground.
> All are equally worthless for all are equally
> fruitless. Fruit-bearing is the whole point of
> agriculture and it is also the ultimate test, then,
> of salvation.

Jesus is warning us in this story that initial professions of faith are a misleading statistic. It is long-term changes in lifestyle, not mere short-term enthusiasm, that really cheer the heart of Christ.

Some well-meaning Christians treat faith like fire insurance. 'Decide for Jesus right now!' they say, 'because once you've paid that single once-in-a-lifetime premium, you have eternal life, and you must never, never doubt it. By this simple step of faith you have guaranteed for yourself admission to heaven absolutely and irrevocably.'

But such a presentation can dangerously distort New Testament Christianity. It leads professing Christians to think they can live the rest of their life as they please. They've made their 'decision for Christ' – so they are safe. They may surrender to all kinds of moral failure or spiritual declension, and yet insist they are 'saved'. Didn't the evangelist tell them that they had eternal life and that they must never doubt it? They had got their fire insurance. They had paid their single lifetime premium. They were, as a result, eternally secure.

Well, the New Testament would not agree. It insists that assurance of eternal salvation is valid only if it is supported by the clear evidence of spiritual growth and productivity. That doesn't mean we are saved by our good works. But it does mean that the only reliable *evidence* of our salvation is *goodness*.

It is those who by persevering produce a crop who are secure, says Jesus. Endurance is the hallmark of the truly converted man or woman. Jesus offers no assurance to the complacency of fruitless branches.

The story is told of how the Victorian preacher Charles Spurgeon, while walking to his church in London, came across a drunk clinging to a lamp-post. 'I'm one of your converts, Mr Spurgeon,' said the drunk.

'You may well be one of *my* converts,' replied Spurgeon, 'but you're certainly not one of *God's* converts, or you wouldn't be in this condition.'

The seed of the Word, when it is savingly received, doesn't just make a temporary impact. It produces enduring change. True faith is not an ephemeral whim in the emotional excitement of an evangelistic meeting. It's not just a nominal nod of the head in the direction of the altar when the Creed is repeated on a Sunday evening. True faith is a deliberate and determined pledge of the heart to a faithful obedience to Christ and his Word, which perseveres through trials and opposition and sustains its growth lifelong. I'm not saying Christians don't have setbacks; of course they do. But they endure. And it is only those who endure to the end who are saved.

There is on the other hand such a thing as an abortive conversion experience, just as there was Judas among the disciples. That's why the New Testament exhorts us:

> *See to it, brothers, that none of you has a sinful, unbelieving heart that turns away from the living God . . . We have come to share in Christ if we hold firmly till the end the confidence we had at first* (Hebrews 3:12, 14).

The kingdom of God begins in our lives when God's rule begins there. And how does God assert his rule in our lives? It is, says Jesus, by the obedient attention we pay to his Word.

2

The meaning of love

Luke 10:25–37

_____

*On one occasion an expert in the law stood up to test Jesus.
'Teacher,' he asked, 'what must I do to inherit eternal life?'*

*²⁶'What is written in the Law?' he replied. 'How do you read
it?'*

*²⁷He answered: '"Love the Lord your God with all your heart
and with all your soul and with all your strength and with all
your mind"; and, "Love your neighbour as yourself."'*

*²⁸'You have answered correctly,' Jesus replied. 'Do this and
you will live.'*

*²⁹But he wanted to justify himself, so he asked Jesus, 'And
who is my neighbour?'*

*³⁰In reply Jesus said: 'A man was going down from
Jerusalem to Jericho, when he fell into the hands of robbers.
They stripped him of his clothes, beat him and went away,
leaving him half-dead. ³¹A priest happened to be going down
the same road, and when he saw the man, he passed by on the
other side. ³²So too, a Levite, when he came to the place and saw
him, passed by on the other side. ³³But a Samaritan, as he
travelled, came where the man was; and when he saw him, he
took pity on him. ³⁴He went to him and bandaged his wounds,
pouring on oil and wine. Then he put the man on his own
donkey, brought him to an inn and took care of him. ³⁵The next
day he took out two silver coins and gave them to the innkeeper.
"Look after him," he said, "and when I return, I will reimburse
you for any extra expense you may have."*

*³⁶'Which of these three do you think was a neighbour to the
man who fell into the hands of robbers?'*

*³⁷The expert in the law replied, 'The one who had mercy on
him.'*

Jesus told him, 'Go and do likewise.'

Judging by the frequency with which the word is celebrated in the Top Twenty, it's quite clear that for many the single answer to the world's troubles is 'love'. And it's not difficult to agree with such a sentiment when you observe what hate does on the world's stage; all the misery it inflicts, the violence it perpetrates, the broken homes, communities, lives and hearts for which it is responsible. It's almost platitudinous to say, in the words of that Beatles song from the 1960s, 'All you need is love.' The problem is, it's one thing to sing about it, and another thing altogether to do it, isn't it?

We all know that love could bring enduring reconciliation in Northern Ireland; it could solve the tensions of the Middle East; it could heal the warring factions of Bosnia and Rwanda. In short, we all know that love could make the whole world go round a great deal more smoothly. The trouble is, we just don't seem to be able to inject enough of this miracle-working moral lubricant into the world's bearings.

Everyone gives assent in principle to the importance of love. But one despairs of finding any out of all the divided peoples of our globe where it is actually being demonstrated. This is nothing new, of course. Two thousand years ago, the thoughtful scribes of Judea had already identified the primary importance of love from their studies of the Bible. But in their case, too, there was a disappointing performance gap between theory and practice. And in Luke 10 Jesus tells a classic story to impress that very point on one learned rabbi with whom he discusses the matter.

The theory of love (Luke 10:25–28)

If you've ever tried your hand at public debate, you'll be familiar with the kind of person who stands up during question time, not with the aim of furthering serious discussion, but simply in order to make a fool of the speaker. When I was at school we had a mock general election, when various senior scholars stood as candidates for the major political parties. I was going through my anarchist phase at that time, so I declined to stand for office myself. But I did gain, I remember, immense satisfaction instead by interrupting every campaign speech I could by demanding in a loud voice, 'What about pig-rearing in the Shetland Islands?' None of the adolescent parliamentarians at my school, I discovered, had given much thought to this serious question. And not a few were reduced to total confusion by being asked to comment on it.

These days, unfortunately, I tend to be on the other end of such subversive tactics. In fact, any church minister who accepts speaking engagements at schools with a preponderance of 'A' level students quickly forms a list of old chestnuts of this sort. Who was Cain's wife? That's a good one. Did Noah have polar bears in the Ark? That's another. One soon learns that people who ask questions like this don't really want an answer, they just want to score points in an intellectual sparring match. It was Martin Luther who executed the most sardonic parry to such an enquiry. He was asked by one garrulous sceptic once, 'What was God doing before he made the world?' To which Luther is reputed to have replied (quoting his own mentor, Augustine), 'Making hell for people who ask stupid questions like that.'

When we read the gospels we discover that Jesus had to cope with a good many such insincere enquirers. Again and again the theologians of his day tried to trap him into making some injudicious comment by which he could be discredited. But it's interesting to observe the way that Jesus refused to be drawn into sterile, speculative arguments. He was, in fact, the master of turning such questions back on the interrogator.

In these verses we find a classic example of Jesus handling just such a would-be controversialist, an expert in the law, Luke calls him, or as we would say, an Old Testament scholar. He raises a query which on the surface sounds guileless enough. Indeed, the man seems to hold Jesus in considerable esteem. He stands to put his question and addresses him respectfully as 'Teacher'. What's more, the enquiry itself appears, superficially at any rate, to be rather promising. 'Teacher,' he says, 'what must I do to inherit eternal life?' But in order that we should not be misled, Luke tells us that his inner motive was rather more disappointing. He stood up, he tells us, to put Jesus to the test.

So this man was not a genuine seeker after spiritual illumination. He was one more of those hostile inquisitors from the Jewish Establishment who were looking for an opportunity to examine Jesus' theological credentials and, if possible, to expose his theological incompetence. No doubt he hoped that Jesus would make some wild messianic claim or utter some heretical statement which could be taken down and used later as evidence against him.

But if so, he was frustrated. For instead of volunteering some theological novelty for him to seize upon, Jesus invited the man to answer his own question from the Old Testament which he knew so well. 'What's written in the Law?' he asked. 'How do you read it?'

And the man was, not surprisingly, only too willing to exhibit the fruits of his biblical research. 'Love the Lord your God,' he said, 'and your neighbour as yourself.'

'You've answered correctly,' Jesus replied.

You may be a little surprised to find this man summarizing the Old Testament law in those terms. For Jesus himself, when asked on another occasion to identify the most important commandment in the Bible, could do no better than to cite precisely the same two texts which this scribe quotes here, namely Deuteronomy 6:5 and Leviticus 19:18, 'Love God. Love your neighbour. The entire moral teaching of the Bible,' he said, 'hinges on these two pivotal imperatives.' (See Matthew 22:34–40.)

So it says much, does it not, for the profundity of this scribe's reflection on biblical ethics, that he had come independently to exactly the same conclusion as Jesus on this point?

Well, actually, no. It probably indicates nothing of the sort. Almost certainly, the fact that the lawyer fastens here on the same two Old Testament quotations as Jesus implies rather that, contrary perhaps to what many of us assume, Jesus was not the first to distil out of these two commandments the essence of God's moral requirement. It seems likely that this scribe's answer represented the conventional wisdom of at least some of the rabbis of Jesus' day. If you had asked any of them, 'What's the essence of the Law? What is the cardinal virtue?' they would have all answered with one voice, 'Love God and love your neighbour.'

And that being so, I suspect this Old Testament expert may have been a little nonplussed when Jesus, this Galilean with such a reputation for radical ideas, applauded his very traditional answer and agreed with its uncontroversial orthodoxy. 'You've answered correctly,' Jesus replied. 'Do this, and you will live.'

Perhaps some of us too are a little disturbed that Jesus should seem to endorse this man's ideas so uncritically. Surely the whole point about Jesus was that he had something new to say about the way to eternal life, something fundamentally contradictory to the Judaism in which this man had grown up. But by replying to him in such a flattering and supportive fashion, it sounds for all the world as if Jesus wants to deny any revolutionary or innovative element in his proclamation of the kingdom of God.

Well, if that's how you're tempted to react, I have to tell you that I think you're making two mistakes.

First, you're misunderstanding the teaching of Jesus. For the New Testament never abrogates the moral demands of the Old Testament law. On the contrary, it everywhere insists that the new-covenant people of God can be identified by their obedience to the moral law which the Holy Spirit works into their lives. When Jesus says, in verse 28, 'Do this and you will live', he's not implying that loving deeds can earn heaven for us; but he is most certainly confirming that loving deeds are the infallible mark of a heaven-bound personality.

This ties in, of course, with the conclusion we drew from the parable of the sower in the last chapter: that you can tell fertile ground which has received the seed of the Word by the moral fruit of obedience to that Word which it bears. This man was effectively asking, 'How can I be certain I belong to the people of God, that I'm one of those who'll inherit the messianic kingdom of God when it arrives?' Jesus' answer is no revolutionary new concept. It is in Deuteronomy just as it is in John. It is in Leviticus just as it is in Romans. 'We know that we have passed from death to life, because we love' (see 1 John 3:14; Romans 13:8–10). Love is the divine requirement. Without it we shall not enter heaven, for heaven is a world of love.

This lawyer, you see, answered better than he knew. People who are going to heaven do love God and their neighbour. The law written on tablets of stone by Moses in the Old Testament, which this man knew so well, is the same moral law which is written on the tablets of the human heart by the Holy Spirit of the new covenant which Jesus had come to inaugurate. As Christ himself said, 'I haven't come to abolish the law, but to fulfil it' (see Matthew 5:17). And love is the fulfilment of the law. In that sense, Jesus is saying nothing at all contradictory to the general tenor of the New Testament when he says, 'Do this, and you will live.'

But I imagine some will still not be satisfied with that. They will object further. 'Oh, that may be so. Moral obedience is the evidence of a spiritually renewed personality. We all know that.' But it is certain that this scribe did not have such a New Testament theological perspective on things. It's quite clear he was spiritually astray, for just look at the way he frames his initial question, 'What must I *do* to inherit eternal life?' Didn't he see the contradiction in his own words? Nobody inherits anything by *doing* things, do they? An inheritance is something you receive by virtue of a relationship, not of an achievement.'

Clearly, like many Jews of this period and many nominal Christians today, this man thought of eternal life as something purchased by his own works of piety rather than given freely by God's grace. It was not a matter of 'What has God done for me?' but rather of 'What must I do for God?' He didn't see love of God and neighbour as the evidential fruit which the Holy Spirit produced in the lives of those who had received eternal life. He saw it as the moral duty which he, by his own unaided efforts, had to perform in order to gain eternal life as a divine reward. That was how his mind worked.

Surely Jesus should have corrected that legalistic self-righteousness underlying the scribe's words? But instead, Jesus seems almost to pat the man on the back and compliment him on his sound approach. 'Do this and you will live.'

'That's not the right answer, Jesus; not for this man! You should have pointed him to faith, not to works, just as Paul does in the letter to the Galatians.' If that's your response, it brings me to the second mistake I think you may be making. Besides perhaps misunderstanding the teaching of Jesus, you may also be underestimating his pastoral wisdom.

Think for a moment about the kind of man this expert in the law was. A professional Bible student, a man who had memorized Genesis to Deuteronomy, who had participated in seminar after seminar of learned debate, sharpening his arguments, clarifying his finer points. A man who had not only examined countless real legal cases but had dreamed up thousands of imaginary ones, so that he could feel absolutely sure that there was no conceivable ethical problem upon which he could not pronounce an authoritative opinion. In short, here was a man with all the answers. Such a person neither needs nor wants theological instruction. That wasn't why he came to Jesus. He had a mind stuffed to the brim with theological instruction, and given half a chance would be only too delighted to parade it for everybody's benefit.

Debate with a person like that is a pointless exercise. It might entertain the crowd, but it's most unlikely to change his mind in any way. Indeed, the philosopher Karl Popper may have been right when he argued that such debate only serves to cement the protagonists ever more securely in their rival positions. Even if Jesus had succeeded in confuting the scribe's theology, he would not have succeeded in converting his soul. He would have won the argument but not the man.

For this fellow needed not to be taught but to be humbled. That first-person pronoun, 'What must I do?' betrayed altogether too much self-confidence. He really thought he could love God and neighbour. That was his most fundamental error; not his legalistic theology, but his moral complacency. The only way this man could be really helped was if that over-confident veneer of smug self-righteousness was punctured by a little bit of old-fashioned conviction of sin.

But as every counsellor knows, conviction of sin cannot be imparted by lecturing people on the subject. When you're seeking to lead a person along the path to repentance, indirect methods are often far more effective than confrontational ones. Jesus, the master psychiatrist, knew that. He would show this man the inadequacy of his theology of good works. But not by scoring a victory over him in theoretical debate; rather, by touching his conscience with a very practical story.

And that brings us to our second parable.

The practice of love (Luke 10:29–35)

It's clear from verse 29 that the lawyer felt that, in spite of Jesus' apparently complimentary response, he had nevertheless somehow experienced a defeat. Perhaps there had been just an edge to Jesus' tone when he said, 'Do this and you will live', as if to imply 'but you don't really love like this, do you?' That certainly seems to be the implication of Luke's observation, that the man felt the need to 'justify himself'. That is, to put himself in the right. The moral challenge of Jesus' words had left him on the defensive. Though nothing explicitly disapproving had been said, he unaccountably felt as though he had been rebuked.

But isn't that how we all feel when someone challenges us with the command to love? G. K. Chesterton once said that Christianity had not been tried and found wanting; it had been found difficult and left untried. That's about the size of it. As we said earlier, everybody agrees that 'Love your neighbour' is fine in theory, but when it comes to practice we find ourselves embarrassed by the unconditional demands such a rule makes upon our lives. Almost unconsciously, we seek to ease the pressure on our consciences, to convince ourselves that in spite of that nagging, uncomfortable feeling of self-reproach, we *do* love our neighbour as ourselves, don't we?

There are two classic ways in which we habitually seek to achieve this sense of self-justification. And it's the genius of Jesus' parable that it unmasks the essential hypocrisy in both of them.

a. The 'I don't do anybody any harm' technique

This first technique is quite simple. You turn God's positive command into a negative prohibition. 'Love your neighbour' is transformed into 'Don't do anybody any harm'. Such passive righteousness is far easier to handle. We can comfort ourselves, since we haven't stolen from, murdered or slandered our neighbour, that we have thereby succeeded in loving him or her. That was clearly the attitude of the priest and the Levite in Jesus' story. I've no doubt these two clergymen were well able to rationalize their decision to pass by on the other side in any number of ways. Just like this lawyer, they could justify themselves.

To begin with, they could claim that it would be *foolish* to stop. This injured man might have been a decoy to trap naïve travellers who let their emotions get the better of their common sense. Then they could argue that it would have been *unbiblical* for them to stop. We are told that the man was 'half-dead', that is, unconscious. For all they knew, he might have been fully dead. If so, then the ceremonial law of the Old Testament forbade any member of the temple staff to go within 6 feet of him. If either of these clergymen had gone over to investigate, only to find they were dealing with a corpse, they would have become ritually defiled. And that would have meant not only going through an irksome procedure of ceremonial cleansing, but being ruled unfit to carry out their liturgical duties for a considerable period of time, to everybody's inconvenience and their considerable embarrassment.

But the chief reason they were able to defend their neglect of this injured man was that their interpretation of the law of love did not *require* them to do anything for him. A passive righteousness that simply refrained from inflicting actual harm on other people was all that was demanded, as far as they were concerned. They hadn't beaten the poor fellow up, had they? Therefore they were not responsible; therefore they didn't have to get involved. That was how their minds worked. Theirs was an ethic which took no account at all of sins of omission, and which could therefore ignore the man without suffering the slightest pang of guilt. 'Why,' they might have said to themselves as they continued down the road, 'he might not even have been a Jew, anyway!'

36

And that brings us to the second strategy of moral evasion.

b. The 'charity begins at home' technique

This technique involves setting limits on the extent of the application of God's command to love. It restricts the operation of that command to a particular group of people who are regarded as the exclusive recipients of the love of which it speaks. 'Who is my neighbour?' our scribe asks, the implication being that some people are my neighbour and some people aren't. He would have taken it for granted that 'Love your neighbour' meant 'Love your fellow Jew'. No rabbi of the day would have suggested anything else. The question in his mind was probably, 'Does that include Gentile converts to Judaism?' because we know that the rabbis were divided on that issue in Jesus' day. Perhaps he thought that by getting Jesus' opinion on that controversy he could generate the academic debate he was seeking. But he can scarcely have been ready for the bombshell that would fall at the very centre of Jesus' story in reply to this technical query.

To understand the emotional impact of verses 33–34 on Jesus' original audience, one needs somehow to get inside the feelings of contempt which Jews entertained towards Samaritans in the first century. The reasons for that contempt we needn't go into. Like all ethnophobia, it was thoroughly irrational. But seldom in the history of the world, I suspect, has there been a racist prejudice that was quite so extreme in the intensity of its mutual loathing.

Unfortunately, this dimension of the story is lost on us. We are so familiar with this parable that the very word 'Samaritan' for us has connotations of benevolence. We all know Samaritans are good. They are those good people who sit on the end of telephones all night long, waiting to counsel potential suicides. But such philanthropic associations were quite foreign to the first-century Jewish mind. On the contrary, in their culture there was no such thing as a 'good Samaritan'. As the American cavalry used to say of the Apaches, the only good Samaritan was a dead Samaritan. And that's no exaggeration. Samaritans were publicly cursed in the synagogues. Petitions were daily offered begging God to deny them any participation in eternal life. Many rabbis even said that a Jewish beggar should refuse alms from a Samaritan because their very money was contaminated.

Jesus could not possibly have chosen a hero more offensive to the sensitivities of his audience. It is not going too far to suggest that he displayed considerable physical courage in doing so. It would be like siding with a black at an Afrikaner brotherhood meeting in Johannesburg. Or like praising a UDR soldier in a Catholic pub in Belfast. If Jesus had made it a Jew helping a Jew, it would have been acceptable. Even a Jew helping a Samaritan might have been tolerable. Some, I'm sure, would have applauded if he'd made his story a piece of anticlerical propaganda, with the Jewish layman showing up the hypocrisy of these two members of the priesthood. But to suggest that two pillars of the Jewish Establishment should be morally outclassed by this mongrel heretic – why, it would have stung every Jewish patriot into hostile indignation! Yet that was exactly Jesus' suggestion.

At every step in the narrative, he makes the Samaritan fulfil the duty of love so conspicuously neglected by the priest and the Levite. Their hearts had been cold and calculating, but his burns with an extravagant compassion. Their oil and wine remain undefiled in their saddlebags, ready, no doubt, for later use in temple ritual. But his becomes a soothing and antiseptic balm to treat the man's wounds. They stay securely seated on their beasts, ready to gallop off should the man's prone body prove to be a decoy. He bravely dismounts, risking possible ambush, and walks the rest of the way to Jericho with the injured man slumped in his own saddle. They kept their money safe in their purse, congratulating themselves, no doubt, on the 10% tithe they had just paid. But he freely sacrifices a month's wages or more in order to secure the nursing care this man would need to make a full recovery.

And note very carefully: all this he did in complete ignorance of the man's racial identity. That is the significance, you see, of Jesus' observation that this man was unconscious and stripped naked. All the normal means by which the ethnic identity of somebody could be established were missing. His dialect and manner of dress were undefined. The Samaritan encounters this victim of criminal violence simply as an anonymous human being. Jew, Gentile, fellow Samaritan – he can't know which. Yet he cares for him. He rescues him. He provides sacrificially for his future welfare. The implication is clear, and Jesus pulls no punches in pointing it out.

The challenge of love (Luke 10:36–37)

You can see the lawyer swallowing hard, can't you, as Jesus forces him to answer his own question again. He can't bring himself to say 'the Samaritan', for that hated word would have stuck in his throat. On the other hand, he can't deny the moral force of the story he's heard. So he replies with embarrassed circumlocution, 'the one who had mercy on him'.

There must have been a glimmer of a smile on Jesus' lips as he observes his discomfiture. This man who had come for a sparring match now finds himself, not just defeated, but convicted. 'Go and do likewise,' is Jesus' call to him (Luke 10:37). And surely in those two imperatives, 'go' and 'do', Jesus unmasks the hypocrisy not only of his original enquirer but also of us all. It is so easy, isn't it, to engage in high-sounding generalizations about loving people. But this masterpiece of a parable grounds the practical implications of that moral theory in real life.

How much are we really prepared to 'go and do' for love of neighbour's sake? it asks.

How much value does love place on a human being? The legalist wants to calculate that sum in very precise terms, so that he might know the limit of his moral duty. 'If I do this much, I have loved.' The effect of that kind of moral computation is to turn love into a very tepid thing; a vague, generalized benevolence which cannot possibly express the infinite preciousness of a human individual at all. We put our subscription in the famine relief fund, we buy our flag from the street collector, and we say, 'There! I've done it. I've loved my neighbour. I've obeyed the command.'

'Rubbish,' says Jesus. 'You haven't even begun yet.' Have you noticed how very careful God is to express his command in the singular? '*You* shall love *your* neighbour.' Love cannot be satisfied with charitable generalities. Says Charlie Brown indignantly in the Peanuts cartoon: 'Of course I love the human race, I just can't stand Lucy.' But Lucy is the measure of love.

Jesus is here concerned to show us that love requires an intensity of preoccupation with an individual. That is love's test. For the human race, we can do very little; that's why it's so easy to say we love them. But there is no limit at all to the lengths to which we might go in showing generosity to specific needy individuals who happen to cross our path, if we value them highly enough.

I'm not denying that the world today is in such great need that bureaucratic charity is necessary. Hungry people have to become statistics on pieces of paper that are passed around desks and offices and through computer memory banks. But be sure of this. That kind of depersonalized care cannot possibly fulfil our obligation to love as God sees it. Real neighbour-love can only flow in the context of a one-to-one, I–thou relationship. For only in such a relationship can the extravagance of love find practical expression.

The gospel of John recounts Judas' irritation when Mary of Bethany, overcome with devotion to the Lord, poured a valuable jar of perfumed ointment at his feet: 'Why wasn't this perfume sold and the money given to the poor?' asked Judas (John 12:5). Notice the phrase 'the poor'. Judas characteristically thought in such categories. Nice, safe, plural, generalized, collective nouns. 'The poor.' But Mary didn't think that way at all. For her, it was Jesus, an individual, a person she loved and would do anything for. Of course it was extravagant. But love *is* extravagant. In vain do you tell the lover, when he looks in the jeweller's window, 'You can't possibly afford that one.' Love sweeps such economic considerations aside. It goes the extra mile, it offers the cloak as well as the coat, it even turns the other cheek. To cold, calculating Judas this was unintelligible and wasteful. But Mary knew that love could not limit itself by degrees. Love is not interested in calculating 'What is the least I can do to fulfil my duty?' It sets such enormous value on a human individual that it must sacrifice anything on his or her behalf. Until it has been so extravagant, it is frustrated and unexpressed.

'Go and do likewise,' says Jesus. 'Next time, Mr Lawyer, you see somebody whom it lies in your power to help, remember my story of the good Samaritan and go and do likewise. Then you'll know what loving your neighbour is all about.'

Must he not say something similar to us? Has he not at a single stroke exposed the fallaciousness of all those clever excuses and rationalizations we use? 'I don't do anybody any harm.' What sort of neighbour-love is that? Such a love would have left this poor man to perish, and congratulated itself on its sound judgment. 'Charity begins at home.' What sort of neighbour-love is that? Had the noble Samaritan himself been the victim in question, such a love would have left him to die and congratulated itself on its moral discrimination.

Jesus' story dramatizes what our consciences already

know, if we were only more honest with ourselves: that when God says 'Love your neighbour' he means a love which willingly engages in positive acts of care and extravagant gestures of self-sacrifice, irrespective of the race, colour or creed of the one in need. A love which refuses to ask, as this lawyer did, 'Who?' but insists on asking only 'How?' A love which is not interested in the possibility of evasion, only in finding opportunity for expression. A love which is not content to be merely applauded theoretically, but which demands to be demonstrated in practice. 'Go and do likewise,' he says.

I'm sure you don't need me to tell you how this world of ours would be turned upside down by such a love. It would work a social transformation far more radical than any economic revolution, whether from the Left or from the Right. Consider the 'charity at home' philosophy, for instance. Take your newspaper and spend a few moments identifying how many of the intractable conflicts, problems and hurts that disturb our world are caused by people asking, just as the lawyer does, 'Who is my neighbour?' We refuse to love with a universal willingness. We consistently adopt a clannishness that discriminates between 'them' and 'us'. Jew and Arab in Palestine, Catholic and Protestant in Northern Ireland, Serb and Croat in the former Yugoslavia, resurgent nationalism in the former Soviet Union, endemic tribalism in black Africa, class prejudice and race prejudice here in Britain – the list goes on and on and on. It doesn't matter which corner of the world you live in, you find neighbour-love perverted by chauvinism and sectarianism into something which isn't love at all, but just an enlightened form of self-interest.

Or consider the 'I don't do anybody any harm' attitude. Hasn't it struck you how much appalling neglect of social responsibility in our modern world is justified by that phrase? Back in 1964, a classic example of this was acted out on the streets of New York. A woman in her late twenties was attacked on her way home by an assailant who stabbed her repeatedly as she screamed for help, and at least thirty-eight people peering through their apartment windows witnessed the crime. Not one even bothered to telephone the police. When they were asked later why they had done nothing, the answer was unanimous: 'We just didn't want to get involved.'

An isolated incident? I'm afraid it isn't. Here's a clip from the *Daily Mail*. 'Motorists slowed down to watch as a man raped a three-year-old girl in broad daylight next to a busy road, but no-one stopped to help her.'

This is the sick world we live in. Jesus' parable is real life today. But in our city centres at night, there are not many good Samaritans around to give the story a happy ending. Our western society has become so preoccupied with its individualistic and materialistic priorities that nobody wants to get involved in anybody else's problem. We just don't do anybody any harm. That's how we comfort ourselves. The victims of crime, of war, of exploitation, of oppression – what business are they of ours? These human tragedies that scar the world aren't our responsibility. So, just like the priest and the Levite, we pass by on the other side, defending ourselves all the time with the excuse, 'We don't do anybody any harm.'

'Whatever you did not do for one of the least of these, you did not do for me' (Matthew 25:45). We have it, then, from the mouth of Christ himself that sins of omission are so heinous, so culpable in God's sight, that they can damn us. For love is the fulfilment of the law. Confronted by the spectacle of human need, love can never stand idly by and do nothing.

I said in the last chapter that it was possible for social concern so to dominate the Christian agenda that we lose sight of the priority of telling the good news of God's kingdom. I don't retract that emphasis. The seed of the kingdom is the Word. But any Christian who fails to demonstrate real social concern in a world like ours, no matter how zealous he may be in his evangelistic endeavour, will face the judgment of Christ. For the seed of the kingdom is the Word, and that very Word demands social concern. Social concern is part of the fruit of obedience which is the evidence of our fertility as soil. John Stott is surely right, then, when he insists that we may not pursue Christ's great commission, 'Go into all the world and preach the good news,' to the neglect of his great commandment. 'My command is this,' he says: 'Love' (Mark 16:15; John 15:12).

There was a time, of course, when the Christian church was, indeed, renowned for its practical obedience to that injunction of the Master. Even unsympathetic critics have to admit that in nineteenth-century England, for instance, it was the Christian believers who toiled indefatigably in the slums for the relief of the poor and the marginalized in society. Would that that were the church's image today! I fear it is not. The virus of individualistic self-indulgence which infects our western society generally is very little resisted by the church today. Like the priest and the Levite, Christians are far more interested in the buzz they get from public worship than in the social responsibility which love demands.

The story of the good Samaritan is as compelling, then, in its relevance to the twentieth-century world and to the twentieth-century church as when Jesus told it 2,000 years ago. Many years ago, I did a Bible study with a small group of students, one of them from Latin America, on this very parable of the good Samaritan. His comment was, 'If only the church had told us this story and demonstrated to us this Jesus, many of my friends would never have become Marxists.' This is, without doubt, one of the most potent recipes for social change the world has ever heard: 'Go and do likewise' (Luke 10:37).

And yet the astonishing irony is this: *that wasn't why Jesus told the story.* Jesus did not tell this parable because he believed it would change the world. Indeed, if he did tell it for that purpose he must be feeling thoroughly disappointed now, 2,000 years on, for it manifestly hasn't.

Now, Jesus is no utopian socialist. Recall again the question with which this whole incident began, for that is the key to it. 'Teacher, what must I do to inherit eternal life?' (Luke 10:25). Here, remember, is a man under the monumental delusion that he can earn his ticket to heaven by good works. And the ultimate purpose of this story is to show that man that he could not. The only reason this scholar could deceive himself into thinking that he could earn his ticket to heaven that way was that he interpreted God's law of love in such a reductionist manner. Once the full extent of his moral obligation is made plain to him, once he examines his life without the fig-leaf of excuses and evasions to hide his failure behind, he quickly discovers that he is not the great moral expert he thought he was. He knows the theory all right, but the practice just isn't there.

We could not be further from the truth, then, when we suggest that Jesus was confirming this man in his Judaistic legalism when he says, 'Do this and you will live' (Luke 10:28). On the contrary, the whole point of his conversation is to strike a hammer-blow at that moral complacency of his.

That's the real reason this story stands in Luke's gospel. We misunderstand it completely if we think its primary purpose is to teach us our moral duty. It is intended, rather, to expose to us our moral bankruptcy. The good Samaritan is Jesus' demolition job on the self-righteousness of those who dare to justify themselves. 'Face up to the performance gap in your life,' the parable says. 'You know God's standards of love, but you don't keep them. Go away and try to keep them if you're so sure you can. But once you stop rationalizing your way out of the full force of God's command, once you stop emasculating the demands of love with comforting clichés like "Charity begins at home", and "I never do anybody any harm", once you start comparing your loving with the extravagant generosity of that good Samaritan of mine, then you will realize what a moral failure you really are. You will not come to me then asking pompous, self-inflated questions like, "What must I do to inherit eternal life?"'

No. Rather, like a man in the next story we shall be looking at, you will be found with your head bowed, beating your breast, saying, 'God be merciful to me, a sinner.' Have you got to that point of self-despair yet? Plenty of people come, like this expert, to have a debate with Jesus. Too few come to him seeking what he really wants to offer – a rescue.

Once we do get to that point where we know we need a rescue, however, we shall discover that there is yet a further dimension to this remarkable story of the good Samaritan; perhaps the most precious dimension of all.

In the last chapter I said that the parables were often abused during the Middle Ages, as a result of the allegorical interpretation of scholars. This story of the good Samaritan suffered more than most in that regard. A typical medieval reconstruction, for instance, tells us that the wounded man represents Adam, and that Jerusalem, from which he journeys, represents the state of innocence from which Adam fell. The thieves who beat him up are the devil who deprived Adam of eternal life. The priest and the Levite are Old Testament religion which passed by and could not help him. And the Good Samaritan, of course, is Christ, who comes to his rescue. The inn to which he takes him is the church; the two coins which are given for his care are the sacraments of baptism and the mass; and the innkeeper, self-evidently, is the pope!

Well, suffice it to say there is no evidence at all that Jesus intended his story to be understood in such a fashion. Yet those medieval scholars were not without their spiritual insight. For even if the good Samaritan was not intended to be an allegorical representation of the mission of Christ, it is true to say that Christ is the perfect fulfilment of the command to love, which the good Samaritan illustrates.

There is a man who travelled that Jericho road, but in the opposite direction: toward Jerusalem, not away from it, and with a cross on his back. And from that cross the Story-teller himself repeats to us that old commandment of love. Only, because he is saying it, it has somehow now also become a new commandment. 'Love one another,' he says, *'as I have loved you'* (see John 13:34). Moses could never have added that second clause, could he? Nor could the lawyer. But Jesus can. For he has turned the good Samaritan from fiction into fact. His is a love that does indeed break down the man-made barriers of race and tribe and class. His is a love that was not satisfied with mere passive goodwill, but insisted upon active, extravagant sacrificial service. 'Love one another,' he says, *'as I have loved you.* You can love that way, now; because, unlike Moses, I have not only brought you the command to love; I have brought you the power to love. My Spirit, poured out from heaven, will reproduce my love in your hearts. Go and do likewise.'

To those who, like this lawyer, think they can earn their ticket to heaven by good deeds, Jesus' words are a challenge to face up to their true moral inadequacy. You don't love like this; you can't love like this. You don't *want* to love like this. Stop fooling yourself.

But to those who have learnt that lesson, who have come to Christ in repentance and faith, confessing their failure and sin, the challenge of these final words comes afresh a second time and with even more force. 'Go and do likewise,' he says. 'Prove the quality of the Spirit-filled life which I have given you. All will know you are my disciples if you love one another as I have loved you.'

3

An invitation to a party

Luke 14:1, 7–24

One Sabbath, when Jesus went to eat in the house of a prominent Pharisee, he was being carefully watched . . .

[7]*When he noticed how the guests picked the places of honour at the table, he told them this parable:* [8]*'When someone invites you to a wedding feast, do not take the place of honour, for a person more distinguished than you may have been invited.* [9]*If so, the host who invited both of you will come and say to you, "Give this man your seat." Then, humiliated, you will have to take the least important place.* [10]*But when you are invited, take the lowest place, so that when your host comes, he will say to you, "Friend, move up to a better place." Then you will be honoured in the presence of all your fellow guests.* [11]*For everyone who exalts himself will be humbled, and he who humbles himself will be exalted.'*

[12]*Then Jesus said to his host, 'When you give a luncheon or dinner, do not invite your friends, your brothers or relatives, or your rich neighbours; if you do, they may invite you back and so you will be repaid.* [13]*But when you give a banquet, invite the poor, the crippled, the lame, the blind,* [14]*and you will be blessed. Although they cannot repay you, you will be repaid at the resurrection of the righteous.'*

[15]*When one of those at the table with him heard this, he said to Jesus, 'Blessed is the man who will eat at the feast in the kingdom of God.'*

[16]*Jesus replied: 'A certain man was preparing a great banquet and invited many guests.* [17]*At the time of the banquet he sent his servant to tell those who had been invited, "Come, for everything is now ready."*

[18]*'But they all alike began to make excuses. The first said,*

"I have just bought a field, and I must go and see it. Please excuse me."

^{19'}Another said, "I have just bought five yoke of oxen, and I'm on my way to try them out. Please excuse me."

^{20'}Still another said, "I have just got married, so I can't come."

^{21'}The servant came back and reported this to his master. Then the owner of the house became angry and ordered his servant, "Go out quickly into the streets and alleys of the town and bring in the poor, the crippled, the blind and the lame."

^{22'}"Sir," the servant said, "what you ordered has been done, but there is still room."

²³"Then the master told his servant, "Go out to the roads and country lanes and make them come in, so that my house will be full. ²⁴I tell you, not one of those men who were invited will get a taste of my banquet."'

Familiarity breeds contempt, they say. In my experience that's certainly true where religion is concerned. The hardest people to talk to about Christian faith are invariably the people who've grown up surrounded by it.

G. K. Chesterton, in this connection, tells a story of a young man who lived centuries ago in the rolling downland of Wessex. He'd heard of a huge white horse which had been mysteriously carved into an unknown hillside by ancient hands. He was so captivated by this rumour that he set off in search of the fabled horse, travelling the length and breadth of the West Country. But, alas, he couldn't find it. At length, weary and disappointed, he returned home, reluctantly concluding that the white horse of his dreams didn't exist, after all. Then, as he surveyed his own village from a distant vantage point, after his long absence, he was astonished to see the object of his quest. The white horse had been there all the time. His village lay at the very centre of it, but he'd never been able to recognize it before, concealed as it was in the familiarity of his environment.

Chesterton, of course, intends that story as an allegory. His point is that there are people (particularly perhaps young people), who set off on an intellectual and spiritual pilgrimage. They have deep questions that they want answered. They visit exotic places looking for answers. They read foreign books; they sample weird experiences. Some travellers may even enrol for outlandish university courses. Deep down this is because they're conscious of some mystery that's summoning them, a holy grail they need to discover. Sadly, in spite of all their efforts, and as time goes by, they become increasingly disillusioned, cynical, agnostic. They don't find the 'white horse' they're seeking.

Perhaps, suggests Chesterton, they need to return home. His logic is that if they did, maybe they would be amazed to find that the answers they're looking for are there already, as close as the Bible on the bookshelf or the church on the street corner. They simply haven't recognized the unique value of these things because they are too commonplace, too familiar. Familiarity breeds contempt.

To try to break down such a wall of indifference, or even contempt, and to help people to discover the novelty and the relevance of the Christian message, is not an easy task. This is especially so when people think they know that message already. It's a bit like the measles vaccination given to babies. All too often a dose of religion, especially if administered in childhood, simply increases your resistance to the real thing when you encounter it later in life. Sunday School classes, unhelpful RE teachers at school, boring morning assemblies in chapel, and, of course, tea parties on the vicarage lawn – they all come back into your mind like a flood, immediately an evangelist stands up to speak. It's like antibodies descending upon some invading virus in your bloodstream. Those memories all conspire to ensure your spiritual immunity to everything that preacher might want to say. Even the best sermons fail to penetrate such defences!

Jesus himself, as a teacher of the good news, experienced just the same problem. Frequently the people he had the hardest trouble with were those with strong religious backgrounds.

Take this incident, for instance. It is the Sabbath day. Jesus has been invited to have a meal at the home of what Luke calls 'a prominent Pharisee'. The scene is a little like those sherry parties that Cambridge college chaplains like to throw after evensong. Everybody is wary of each other, and trying hard to make a good impression. It looks as though Jesus, observing the pretentiousness of this particular gathering, had decided that he would liven things up a little. He offers some controversial advice on how to organize a really good dinner party. Don't invite wealthy friends and neighbours, he suggests. That's really naff and boring. After all, if you do that, they'll simply feel obliged to invite you back again, won't they? Instead, invite the homeless youngsters you see begging on the High Street. Invite the alcoholics and the drug addicts you see propped against the wall in the shopping mall. Invite the outcasts and the destitute to your party, because they haven't got a penny. The only reward you can expect if you invite them will be in heaven, won't it?

These words of Jesus must have fallen like a lead balloon on this particular gathering. It doesn't take much imagination to realize what a conversation-stopper it must have been. Outcasts and destitute people, one suspects, were conspicuous by their absence from this prominent Pharisee's respectable table. No doubt there was an embarrassed silence. It was a bit like being reminded of the starving millions when you're just about to dive into your third helping of Black Forest gateau. Of course, there is always someone around at awkward moments like that who considers it his bounden duty to ease the atmosphere by making some inane comment or other. There was just such a fellow at Jesus' table. Determined to keep the conversation within everybody's comfort zone, he nods sanctimoniously at Jesus' allusion to the resurrection of the righteous and adds his own plaudit. 'Blessed is the man,' he says, 'who will eat at the feast in the kingdom of God' (Luke 14:15).

This was merely a conventional platitude, the kind of empty cliché that you hear at funerals when people don't really know what to say, but feel they must say something religious. 'Ah, well, vicar, he's gone to a better place now. What is it that old hymn says? There is a happy land far, far away.' You know the kind of thing. In first-century Jewish society, the rabbis talked a great deal about the coming kingdom of God. Prophets like Isaiah had likened it to a huge free feast laid on by God himself that would make even the most lavish banquet at Buckingham Palace look meagre and parsimonious by comparison. So if you were a first-century party-goer, and short of something sufficiently pious to say in the company of clergymen, a useful standby was, 'Blessed is he who will eat at the feast in the kingdom of God.' This immediately marked you out as a respectable supporter of the ecclesiastical *status quo*. It was a coded way of saying, 'Oh, you don't have to worry about me, Jesus, I'm very religious.'

And, no doubt, the man expected an equally conventional reply as a result; the first-century Jewish equivalent of 'Amen, brother! Hallelujah!' perhaps, followed by a rapid change of subject to something a little more conducive to the digestion of Black Forest gateau. But if so, he gravely miscalculated. Jesus was far too shrewd to be deceived by his unctuous piety, and far too good a pastor to allow it to pass unchallenged.

You see, it was a classic case of familiarity breeding contempt. This fellow thought he was spiritually OK. He knew about and believed in heaven, and was quite sure he was going there. He naturally assumed Jesus would want to support him in this confidence. But, interestingly, Jesus doesn't. The master teacher had a special weapon in his armoury of rhetoric with which to prick the bubble of this kind of religious complacency. We saw him wield it against that lawyer in the last chapter. Here he displays it once again, to devastating effect; a parable with a sting in its tail.

> *A certain man was preparing a great banquet and invited many guests . . .* (Luke 14:16).

This fellow was looking forward to the heavenly banquet secure in the knowledge that he would be there. He's waiting for a conventional reply to his conventional cliché about the blessing of the heavenly feast. And as Jesus begins to tell his story he must feel reassured that that is exactly what he is going to get.

By speaking of a great banquet Jesus is clearly taking up this well-known metaphor of the kingdom of God to which his fellow guest had already referred. The story opens, you will notice, with preparations for the coming feast already well under way. Guests have received their invitations. Jesus' audience would have no trouble decoding this. It is clearly a reference to the preparatory work of the Old Testament prophets who had given preliminary notification of the kingdom's future arrival. As for these guests who had been invited, they (of course) were the Jews, God's chosen people to whom the prophets had addressed their inspired words. No doubt Jesus' audience anticipated that the story was going to go on, through its extended metaphor, to expound the bliss of the kingdom of God, to describe how rich the menu would be, perhaps, or how honoured the guests.

But at this point Jesus' story starts to take a less conventional line.

At the time of the banquet he sent his servant to tell those who had been invited, 'Come, for everything is now ready' (Luke 14:17).

In the ancient world a host would often invite guests a day or two before a feast so that he could determine how many to cater for. Then, when the food was prepared for the expected number, he would send a second invitation summoning his guests to come without further delay. In his story Jesus exploits that contemporary protocol, but in doing so he injects a slightly unexpected note of urgency and imminence. 'Come, for everything is now ready,' the host in the story urges. If they had thought about it (and I'm sure their minds were working overtime to try to do so), Jesus' audience couldn't miss the implication of that. The ancient prophets had announced the coming of the kingdom in the future tense. But Jesus here is suggesting that a new stage in God's timetable has been reached. God is now sending a servant to announce, not that the kingdom of God *will* come at some future date, but that it *has already come.* The banquet is ready; the kingdom is here; it's time, therefore, to act. 'Come, for everything is now ready.'

Who is this servant, charged with so revolutionary a message? I don't think there can be any doubt that Jesus has introduced himself into his parable here. For this was precisely the role he understood God to have given him, his unique messianic mission. He had not simply come to prophesy about the coming kingdom of God, but to inaugurate it! And before Jesus' audience can recover from this startling claim implicit within his words, the Stealth bomber starts dropping its cargo.

But they all alike began to make excuses. The first said, 'I have just bought a field, and I must go and see it. Please excuse me.'

Another said, 'I have just bought five yoke of oxen,

and I'm on my way to try them out. Please excuse me.'

Still another said, 'I have just got married, so I can't come.'

Here is an astonishing suggestion: that people could be personally invited to share in the kingdom of God, and yet decline. Even from a friend, an invitation to dinner isn't lightly turned down. To refuse God's invitation, however, is not just folly, but downright insolence.

It might not have been so bad if these people had dreamed up some good excuse. But the pretexts upon which they made their refusal were so feeble and contrived as to be quite insulting. Can you imagine anybody buying a house without going to look at it first? No more could any first-century Jew imagine someone buying ten oxen without seeing whether or not any of them were crippled. Can you imagine anybody getting married at such short notice that they have to cancel a dinner engagement made a day or two before, so that they can go on their honeymoon? Still less could a first-century Jew, for whom a wedding was something planned months ahead, imagine such a thing!

Every one of these excuses is a transparent fabrication, a deliberate slap in the face. They don't even pretend to be real excuses. Each of these people, in their own way, is saying to their would-be host: 'Frankly, old chap, there are lots of things I'd much rather be doing with my time than spending it in your company.'

'Dinner is ready, you say? Yes, I know I said I'd come, but that was yesterday, old man. I'm terribly sorry to say I've just decided I need to repaint the bathroom tonight.'

'Dinner is ready? Well, yes, I know I said I'd come, but that was yesterday, old man. I'd decided to go for a little spin in the sports car this evening instead; the weather's so nice.'

'Dinner is ready? Well, yes, I know I said I'd come, but

that was yesterday, old man. Please forgive me; I've made a date with this delicious blonde from the office, and you know what they say about "two's company"?'

None of Jesus' hearers could fail to detect the outrageous impertinence of such excuses.

And Jesus of course is suggesting by means of his parable that men and women turn their backs on the kingdom of God with just the same insolence. They do so for the sake of mere trivialities, the pursuit of material gain, personal pleasure, or sexual adventure. They choose such things rather than accept God's invitation. Don't they realize what they're missing? Alas, the implication of Jesus' story is that all too often familiarity breeds contempt. There are far too many counter-attractions bidding for the time and attention of these people. They may have been interested in going to the party once, but all sorts of other things have invaded their life since then.

One suspects that at this point Jesus' story was beginning to get uncomfortably close to the bone for some in his audience. The Stealth bomber had indeed penetrated their defences and had dropped its load. But Jesus wasn't finished. In a final *coup de grâce* he goes on to press the detonator.

> *The servant came back and reported this to his master. Then the owner of the house became angry and ordered his servant, 'Go out quickly into the streets and alleys of the town and bring in the poor, the crippled, the blind and the lame.'*
>
> *'Sir,' the servant said, 'what you ordered has been done, but there is still room.'*
>
> *Then the master told his servant, 'Go out to the roads and country lanes and make them come in, so that my house will be full. I tell you, not one of those men who were invited will get a taste of my banquet'* (Luke 14:21–24).

Do you see what I mean about a sting in the tail? '. . . Not one of those men who were invited will get a taste of my banquet.' To get the point, we must ask ourselves: 'Who were these original invited guests? Who did they represent?' The answer, of course, is the Jews, the religious people, the Bible-believing people, those who saw themselves *en route* to heaven, like Jesus' smug colleague at the Pharisee's dinner party. Yet, in this scorching punch-line, Jesus concludes: 'Not one of those men who were invited will get a taste of my banquet.'

Can he be serious? He's implying that the religiously privileged will be excluded from the kingdom of God. Who then is to be included? 'Go out quickly into the streets and alleys of the town and bring in the poor, the crippled, the blind and the lame.' Here were the very same outcast and destitute beggars, the poor and the disadvantaged, whom Jesus advised the Pharisees to invite to their dinner party, but who were conspicuous by their absence at that particular table. Such people will be there at God's banquet, affirmed Jesus. And, as if their admission to the kingdom were not offensive enough to Jesus' respectable audience, he adds: 'But there is still room.' Then, says the master, 'Go out to the roads and country lanes and make them come in.'

It is possible, of course, that this second sending out of the servant just reinforces the first, thus intensifying the humiliation for Jesus' audience. Most commentators agree, however, that Jesus is doing a little more than that. He's anticipating the incorporation of the Gentiles into the kingdom of God. The gospels certainly teach that Jesus did foresee such a development. 'The kingdom of God will be taken away from you and given to a people who will produce its fruit,' he told some chief priests and Pharisees a little later (Matthew 21:43). Though admittedly it's not absolutely clear from this parable, it does seem likely that those in the roads and country lanes represent non-Jewish outsiders whom Jesus would soon draw to himself by his Spirit after his death and resurrection.

The irony, then, could not be more complete. Those who were expecting to enter the kingdom because they had received advance invitations through the prophets would miss out. But those who expected to be shut out because they were not good enough, or had never even heard of the banquet because they were downright pagans, would be the ones to enjoy it.

Familiarity, this parable emphasizes, does indeed breed contempt, and Jesus responds that contempt is a sin that God does not lightly forgive.

What does the sting in the tail of this parable mean for you and me, then? Perhaps it depends on where we're coming from. Some, like Jesus' dinner guests at that Pharisee's table, come from a religious background. We may have been baptized or dedicated as children by believing parents. Maybe we attended Sunday School or church youth clubs. We may have made some response to gospel meetings in our early teens. We may have heard the Christian faith set out, not once but dozens of times, and as a result we think we're Christians. But are we? That's the question this parable puts to us. We may know how to say grace before meals, but Jesus is saying that the kingdom of God demands more of us than pious platitudes. It demands decision and commitment. 'Come,' he says, 'for everything is now ready.' There was, maybe, a time when you could mark time spiritually, but now that Jesus has come, an active response is required, for the kingdom is here. That kingdom must take precedence over all the other interests and ambitions we have. Are we ready to accept such a radical reorientation of our priorities? he asks. The warning of his story is that many are not. Not everybody who hears the invitation, or even everyone who shows some initial response to the invitation, actually comes up with the goods when decision and commitment are required of them.

For some, perhaps, it's career that takes first place; for others it may be sport; for some it could be the pursuit of academic study; for others it may be a boyfriend or a girlfriend. I have bought a field; I have bought five yoke of oxen; I have married a wife. The excuses change, and yet, in another sense, they are always the same – feeble, contrived, and as far as God is concerned, downright insulting.

Jesus says of such excuses: 'Then the owner of the house became angry.' This is not surprising. If you'd gone to great pains to prepare a banquet for much-valued friends, and they turned their backs on it, wouldn't you be angry? It is naïve to think that God is not angry with us when we find excuses for putting other things before him in our lives. It cost God a lot to lay this banquet of his kingdom before us. He had to pay a price to open the door of heaven for us. A cross stood on a Jerusalem hillside, stained with blood. It stood there so that we could be absolutely sure that this banquet, though free, was not cheap. He paid that price because he wanted to invite you to the banquet. Turn your back on the invitation and you slap the face of a divine host who has given everything because he loves you. No wonder he's angry.

So there is a solemn warning here in this parable for those who are familiar with Christian faith: don't let that familiarity breed contempt. But the parable also carries a very strong encouragement for people without a religious background. God is planning a party for you. All the jubilees and carnivals, banquets and fiestas, laughter and festivity of a thousand years of human history won't compare with the wonder, the glory and joy of the celebration which the King of the universe has on schedule. It will be a magnificent occasion, beyond human imagination, the prelude to a whole new world. Who wouldn't like to be part of that celebration? Jesus tells us, in this parable, that you are invited to it.

Admission is free and each of us is welcome to share in it.

Perhaps for some this is a problem. As the poor, the crippled, the blind and the lame felt out of place at a Pharisee's table, so they feel like a fish out of water in church. 'I'm not the religious type,' they say. 'It's no good these church-goers inviting *me* to become a Christian; they don't know what I'm like. If they did know, they'd immediately show me the door. I'm just not good enough. If they knew what a mess I'd made of my life, if they knew all the habits and sins hidden beneath this polite and respectable exterior of mine, they would know I could never become a Christian. There can be no place for me in Jesus' kingdom of God. The invitation can't be for me.'

Alternatively, like those in the roads and country lanes who didn't even know the banquet had been arranged, some may feel completely bewildered by Jesus' invitation. Perhaps they come from a culture completely alien to Christianity; a country where another religion altogether claims the allegiance of the majority of the people. 'It's all very well for Europeans and Americans to think they're invited to this party,' they say to themselves. 'It can't be for me. I'm from Asia (or Africa). I'm a Hindu (or a Muslim). Me a Christian? That's impossible; unthinkable. There can't be any place for me in Jesus' kingdom. The invitation can't be for me.'

But Jesus in fact tells this story precisely to point out that you are wrong to feel excluded in that way. This story reveals that there is more room in the kingdom of God for people like you than for anybody else. Notice the word the host uses to command the servant: 'Go out to the roads and country lanes and *make them come in*' (Luke 14:23). The verb 'make' is a very strong one. Some translations render it, 'Compel them to come in.' Translated like that, it has occasionally led to illegitimate conclusions, as when it was quoted to defend the Spanish Inquisition.

But such applications fail to understand the function of this strong injunction to the servant. He is not being sent out with ropes, chains and machine guns to drag reluctant strangers back to his master's house! That isn't what the master means when he says, 'Compel them to come in.' The master's command is born of his recognition that the people he's sending the servant to reach out to will be utterly surprised when they receive the invitation. Their immediate reaction will be that the servant has got it wrong; the banquet can't be for them. They will feel that they are far too poor to be invited to a great house like that of the servant's master. They will feel that as Gentiles or strangers, they can't be intended as guests. The invitation must have been delivered to the wrong house. Hence the master says, 'Make them come in.' He means, grab them by the arm, persuade them, convince them, cajole them even. The servant is to use all the means at his disposal to assure them that the host's invitation really does include them. And that's why we can be so confident that God's invitation includes us, whoever we are. It is not qualified or limited by 'ifs' and 'buts'. No matter how unworthy we may feel, no matter how 'un-Christian' and alien, the invitation is for all. *You* are invited. God wants *you* in his kingdom. He urges *you* to come along; the party is ready for *you* now. Why delay?

No doubt we have our plans for the coming months and years. Perhaps a student is studying for a degree. What is he going to do then? Perhaps another has found someone she wants to marry. What about when the wedding is over? Maybe they have ideas about a career. Maybe they are planning to have a family. But the career will end and the children will grow up. What then?

The truth is that however much you can cram into these fifty, sixty, seventy, eighty years that God has given you, it only ends in one place. The estate or the five yoke of oxen we've just bought, even the wife we've just married, seems so very important to us. And of course, they are, in their way. But none of it lasts. It all ends in a wooden box with brass handles and a small engraved name-plate.

In contrast, what Jesus is speaking about here will last for ever. He's concerned about the kingdom of God, something we human beings were designed to share with our Maker. We are meant to live for ever in God's company in God's world. Even though we've thrown that unique destiny away, he's giving us a chance to have it back again! Are we going to turn our backs on such a prospect yet again?

By all means study for your degree, but study for it for him. You may well get married one day, but that home you build can be a home for him. Certainly you'll have a career; make it a career for him. Come, he says, the kingdom is ready, and it's waiting for you. You can start putting up the decorations for the party even now. God wants you to use the life he's given you to prepare for a kingdom that will last for ever.

So why delay? Come, he says. Everything is now ready. No matter how unworthy and alien you feel in respect of this Christianity business, the invitation is for you. If you're already familiar with the invitation, be warned. Familiarity can breed contempt. The invitation can be refused, neglected, forfeited. And the people who are most in danger of that are the people who know it all already. There are no exceptions to Jesus' imperative: 'Seek first the kingdom of God,' he says. He insists that there will be no place at all in that kingdom for those who make feeble excuses for putting it second to anything.

4

Getting lost and losing out

Luke 15:1–2, 11–32

Now the tax collectors and 'sinners' were all gathering round to hear him. ²But the Pharisees and the teachers of the law muttered, 'This man welcomes sinners, and eats with them' . . .

¹¹Jesus continued: 'There was a man who had two sons. ¹²The younger one said to his father, "Father, give me my share of the estate." So he divided his property between them.

¹³'Not long after that, the younger son got together all he had, set off for a distant country and there squandered his wealth in wild living. ¹⁴After he had spent everything, there was a severe famine in that whole country, and he began to be in need. ¹⁵So he went and hired himself out to a citizen of that country, who sent him to his fields to feed pigs. ¹⁶He longed to fill his stomach with the pods that the pigs were eating, but no-one gave him anything.

¹⁷'When he came to his senses, he said, "How many of my father's hired men have food to spare, and here I am starving to death! ¹⁸I will set out and go back to my father and say to him: Father, I have sinned against heaven and against you. ¹⁹I am no longer worthy to be called your son; make me like one of your hired men." ²⁰So he got up and went to his father.

'But while he was still a long way off, his father saw him and was filled with compassion for him; he ran to his son, threw his arms around him and kissed him.

²¹'The son said to him, "Father, I have sinned against heaven and against you. I am no longer worthy to be called your son. [Make me like one of your hired men.]"

²²'But the father said to his servants, "Quick! Bring the best robe and put it on him. Put a ring on his finger and sandals on his feet. ²³Bring the fattened calf and kill it. Let's have a feast and celebrate. ²⁴For this son of mine was dead and is alive

again; he was lost and is found.' So they began to celebrate.

[25]'Meanwhile, the older son was in the field. When he came near the house, he heard music and dancing. [26]So he called one of the servants and asked him what was going on. [27]"Your brother has come," he replied, "and your father has killed the fattened calf because he has him back safe and sound."

[28]'The older brother became angry and refused to go in. So his father went out and pleaded with him. [29]But he answered his father, "Look! All these years I've been slaving for you and never disobeyed your orders. Yet you never gave me even a young goat so I could celebrate with my friends. [30]But when this son of yours who has squandered your property with prostitutes comes home, you kill the fattened calf for him!"

[31]'"My son," the father said, "you are always with me, and everything I have is yours. [32]But we had to celebrate and be glad, because this brother of yours was dead and is alive again; he was lost and is found."'

———————————

When personal relationships break down it's usually by one of two routes.

Sometimes relationships are blown apart by 'the big row'. In a marriage, perhaps, it's the discovery of an adulterous affair that is the trigger. In an ordinary friendship it might be some other kind of dispute or injury that inflames tempers. But whatever the precise details, the resulting rift is sudden and explosive. One party tells the other, 'I never want to see you again. Drop dead. Get lost.' Anyone who has experienced this kind of rift in a relationship knows well enough how traumatic it feels. It is like a bereavement. A person you have loved is suddenly snatched from your side, leaving an aching void, which often fills up with bitterness, and certainly with loneliness. It's a shattering experience, and all the more shattering because it erupts into our life with so little warning. One minute everything seems fine, and then the next our whole world has fallen apart.

Devastating though that kind of relational breakdown

is, however, it's not the only way it happens, nor is it the most hopeless. Sometimes relationships simply drift apart. There's no single crisis that precipitates this parting of the ways. The emotional disengagement is gradual, so gradual you almost don't notice it happening. The marriage doesn't shatter because of the assault of some external sexual temptation; it dies imperceptibly from within. The friendship isn't terminated overnight. It slides by degrees into mutual indifference. Affection cools, communication dries up, until one day we realize we've become strangers to one another; not so much hostile as apathetic; not so much angry as frigid – because this isn't 'the big row', but the 'slow freeze'. When relationships disintegrate in this second way, there's no volcanic disturbance. The result can be just as tragic and as emotionally impoverishing. We may not have told the other person to get lost, but we lose out just the same, and perhaps even more irretrievably. At least, that's the warning which Jesus seems to be giving in his story of the prodigal son. It is perhaps the most famous story he ever told.

It is important to notice the very beginning of the chapter in which Luke records it.

> *Now the tax collectors and 'sinners' were all gathering round to hear [Jesus]. But the Pharisees and the teachers of the law muttered, 'This man welcomes sinners, and eats with them'* (Luke 15: 1–2).

This scene-setting paragraph is an indispensable clue to the meaning of the story which follows. It provides its social context; a division between two classes of people in Jewish society in the first century. On the one hand there were the 'sinners'; on the other the 'saints'. 'Sinners' is perhaps an unfairly pejorative title; not everybody in this class was categorized thus because of some personal moral failing on their part. It could simply be that they had Gentile blood, or had contracted some illness like leprosy, which made them ritually unclean. But it has to be said that a fairly high proportion of those who would have been called 'sinners' in first-century Jewish society were so called as a result of their chosen lifestyle. Some of them, perhaps, were drunkards; some of them might have been sexually immoral; others were tax collectors, corrupt collaborators with the detested occupying army of Rome. Quite a few were the sort of people who didn't go to church on Sunday, but went down the pub instead. Others didn't pray on their knees; they preyed on their neighbours. As you might expect, respectable religious people in Israel gave all such 'sinners' the cold shoulder; they were outcasts. To keep company with such people was to be defiled by them; to be, as we would say, tarred with the same brush. Religious people saw themselves as the 'saints'. They were racially pure Jews, physically whole – no leprosy or anything like that about them – and morally impeccable. The 'saints' kept God's law to the letter, studying their Bibles with a zeal that would put many Christians to shame, and observing it with a rigid and uncompromising pedantry.

Chief among these 'saints' were the Pharisees and the teachers of the law. The Pharisees were a first-century fundamentalist club. The teachers of the law were professional Bible scholars. Between them they constituted a formidable spiritual élite, possessing huge social prestige, and not inconsiderable political power in first-century Judea, where religion was part of the structure of society in a way that it's long since ceased to be in most western countries. Naturally they assumed that any Bible teacher would seek their seal of approval. The last thing they expected of a would-be rabbi like Jesus was that he would abandon the company of the saints altogether in order to socialize with the first-century equivalent of the local rugby club. But that's what Jesus did. Oblivious to the consequences it would have for his reputation, he not only welcomed these so-called 'sinners', he dined with them, to the shock and amazement of all concerned. 'Can you imagine anything so disgusting?' the 'saints' would be saying to one another. In twentieth-century terms, it would be a little like seeing Mother Teresa in a singles' bar in Soho, or Cliff Richard on a gay pride march; it would awaken that same kind of bewilderment. To mix with sinners was totally out of keeping with social expectation for a man who claimed to be holy.

For the disjuncture between 'saints' and 'sinners' in the minds of those religious leaders of the first century was absolute. By flouting this social taboo, Jesus, as it eventually turned out, was in fact signing his own death warrant.

But he was not embarrassed or apologetic about this social policy of his. On the contrary, this wasn't the first time he had deliberately scandalized the religious Establishment in Judea. As we saw in the previous chapter, he had caused similar controversy at a dinner party thrown by a prominent Pharisee. And on that occasion his response to the sanctimoniousness of those around him had been to tell a parable which, like a Cruise missile, penetrated the psychological defences of his hostile audience and enabled him to assault some of their most cherished and preconceived ideas.

Jesus' strategy here is just the same. He finds himself under attack for his policy of eating with 'sinners', so he again tells a parable. Indeed, it is not a single parable this time, but three parables: the parables of the lost sheep, of the lost coin, and of the lost son. It's that third and final story, the most famous story Jesus ever told, that deserves special attention.

It's a story about relationships, a triangle of domestic tension between a father and two sons. In each case the relationship is broken. Each boy, at least for part of the story, is isolated. In one case, this happens as a result of a big row. In the other case it happens as a result of a 'slow freeze'. Interestingly, the son who is alienated from his father by the first route, through the big row, is eventually reconciled to him. For the second boy, outside the circle because of a slow freeze, the story ends in an open-ended way. When the curtain comes down we don't know whether or not he is ever fully reconciled to his father and his brother.

As with all of Jesus' parables, underneath the surface detail there is a spiritual message. Jesus is making the point that our relationship with God is like that between the father and his two boys. Some people's rebellion against God is open and defiant. They are 'sinners' who have a big row with God, angrily turning their backs on him. Others, who like perhaps to think of themselves as the 'saints', still rebel, but secretly, and in a disguised fashion. They maintain a polite, nodding acquaintance with God, but they are careful that he never gets too close. Underneath there is a coldness of heart – a slow freeze.

Jesus' warning is very simple. The 'sinners' have the better chance of going to heaven. This is because people who see themselves in that class have a position that is retrievable. The so-called 'saints', on the other hand, will discover that their smug self-righteousness has placed them beyond hope of redemption.

> *There was a man who had two sons. The younger one said to his father, 'Father, give me my share of the estate.' So he divided his property between them* (Luke 15:11–12).

Here is a classic example of the big row. The story is a familiar one. A teenage boy rebels against his wealthy father. In days like ours, where such family disputes are commonplace, you will find many young kids of sixteen or seventeen sleeping in city parks with a story like this to tell. And for that reason, it's easy perhaps for the scandalous nature of what this boy is suggesting here to lose its impact on us. Even today in a middle-eastern context, what this boy was asking of his father was scandalous and preposterous. To demand his inheritance in advance amounted to saying that he wished his father were dead. Indeed, I suspect, for Jesus' audience the impertinence of this boy's request would have been exceeded only by their astonishment at the father's acquiescence. 'So he divided his property between them.' What sort of parent is this, who accedes to his children's reckless demands for truant independence?

The answer is, of course, a divine parent, for this is a parable. Jesus is drawing a picture for us here of how human beings, made in the image of God, find themselves alienated from him as a result of their moral rebellion. We say to God, 'I wish you were dead.' While we like the material things which he can give us, we don't like *him*. We want *them*, but we don't want *him*. We wish him to get out of our lives, to stop interfering with us.

Ironically, as the story goes on to point out, we are the ones who lose out every time we say that.

> Not long after that, the younger son got together all he had, set off for a distant country and there squandered his wealth in wild living. After he had spent everything, there was a severe famine in that whole country, and he began to be in need. So he went and hired himself out to a citizen of that country, who sent him into his fields to feed pigs. He longed to fill his stomach with the pods that the pigs were eating, but no-one gave him anything (Luke 15:13–16).

What was this young fellow looking for? 'Freedom' is a word we often bandy around: freedom from moral inhibitions, freedom from the shackles of outmoded conventions, freedom from our parents' cramping life-style. We need freedom to discover our real identities. But when this boy found freedom, it was a more complicated thing than he thought.

Imagine someone on the top of a cliff. He feels he's free. 'Free to jump, free to fly like a bird.' So he launches himself off the cliff, and flies like a bird – all the way to the bottom! He failed to appreciate the gravity of the situation! Some of us spend quite a bit of time clearing up the mangled mess at the bottom of that particular cliff of 'freedom'.

Freedom, you see, is not the licence to do as we like. Properly understood, freedom is the liberty to do as we ought, the freedom to be what we were meant to be. We human beings are not unconstrained creatures; there are norms within which we are intended to operate. Without those norms freedom is meaningless, indistinguishable from the arbitrariness of a person who just makes decisions by tossing coins all the time. That boy may have been looking for freedom, but he didn't find the freedom he was looking for when he broke free from his father. All that he found was the stink of a pigsty. In the story of this dissatisfied, degraded individual, Jesus illuminates the tragedy of all of us when we, in our folly, try to be free in an impossible way. We are not the captains of our own souls. We are made by God and cannot escape that creatureliness, no matter how hard we flap our wings on the edge of the cliff.

The words 'no-one gave him anything' are full of pathos. He no doubt found plenty of people willing to exploit his hunger, but they were all takers, not givers. The same is true today, of course. Some drug-pusher will be looking for some such young rebel out on the streets tonight. He's not really interested in him, only his money. He wants to see him feeble, wretched, and begging for the next fix. He's not a giver, but a taker. The same goes for the prostitute. She tells us that sex is the answer, and promises to give us love. The truth is that she doesn't give at all; hers is simply another kind of taking. The same goes for the New Age guru who offers his (expensive) lectures on meditation. All alike assure us that they are here to give us answers to our spiritual quest, but they are not givers, only takers.

Imagine this boy, then, hungry in his pigsty. Maybe you don't need to imagine the scene. You have had your fling in search of freedom, and it has turned to ashes in your mouth too. Deep down you have a gnawing vacuum, just like the hole in this boy's stomach. Jesus explains why this is. It has come about because we are off the track, trying to be something we can't be, that is, free from God. We are flouting the norms of human existence, and our situation isn't going to get any better till we face up to it. This young fellow, mercifully, did.

> When he came to his senses, he said, 'How many of my father's hired men have food to spare, and here I am starving to death! I will set out and go back to my father and say to him: Father, I have sinned against heaven and against you. I am no longer worthy to be called your son; make me like one of your hired men' (Luke 15:17–19).

At last the boy starts to do something right for a change. The first thing he does right is easily overlooked. He refuses to eat the pig food. Jesus' story tells us quite explicitly that he was inclined to eat it; when you're very hungry you'll eat anything. But if his hunger had led him to such a degraded appetite, if he had been satisfied with the second best, what a tragedy it would have been. That choice was a real danger, of course. Many people get to the point of desiring some deeper meaning in life, and even search a little for it. In fact, most people do so at some point in their life. But many, finding no immediate (or perhaps no palatable) answer, settle for second best.

They eat the pig food that's on offer and make their home in the pigsty.

I get the impression that when I was a student in the 1960s we were far more interested in social affairs than students today. We went out and about, waving our banners, staging our sit-ins and protest rallies. Quite a few of my friends waved the red flag of Marxism and the black flag of anarchism. But most of them are now in the City of London, as bank managers, stockbrokers, or something similar. A great hero of ours, I remember, was one of those South American revolutionary types; he ended up opening a boutique in Paris. Disillusionment and cynicism have a way of creeping in and corroding our youthful idealism. We discover that our revolutions don't work the way they were intended, and the result is that we give in to the materialism we said we despised so much. Our spiritual hunger for something better and nobler withers.

The strange thing about this boy's hunger is that it was also his hope. Had he eaten the pig food, all would have been lost. The first thing he did right was to refuse to dehumanize himself in that way. He decided to stay hungry. He opted to go on thinking and searching, in spite of the emptiness that was gnawing at his soul. The most tragic thing about many people in this world is that they are in the pigsty, eating the pig food, and oblivious to the fact. They have stopped looking for anything better.

But of course that momentous refusal wasn't enough. Not only did the boy refuse to eat pig food, he also took a long hard look at his situation, and faced up to some unpleasant truths. It takes courage to look in the mirror and accept what you see. None of us likes doing that – for we live a lot closer to despair than perhaps we can afford to admit. To surrender our precious delusions, to admit that deep down inside we are falling apart and don't know where we're going, to stop playing a role and be real with ourselves – that is brave. Most of us hide our uncertainty about ourselves behind a mask. For some of us the mask is that of the cool academic type; for others the muscular, athletic type. For some it's the 'girl who knows how to handle boys' type, for others the shy, lovable type. For some, it's the 'life and soul of the party' type, for others the aloof, detached, 'I don't need anybody' type. Some people even develop a kind of schizophrenia, adopting different roles depending on where they are and who they're with. I find this happening with some students I know in Cambridge, who have one mask for home and one for university, one for church and one for college. Fundamentally it's a sign of insecurity; they don't know who they really are, or want to be, or are meant to be. Such people are confused about their identity, as this boy was confused. Tragically, some never get beyond that role-play. As they get older the roles change, but the masks become even more firmly fixed to their faces. Eventually the masks never come off, not even in those quiet, private moments when there's nobody there to see them.

To get away from the audience and to engage in radical self-examination marked an indispensable step in this boy's salvation. This is the point Jesus is making. The same courage is required of us if we're going to get out of the hole we're in. We must face up to certain truths, according to Jesus.

The first truth is that we are *lost*. Our lives are dissatisfied and unhappy basically because of this. The root of his problem dawned on this boy as he sat there in his pigsty: it was not that he lacked something called food. Rather he lacked someone called 'father'. Augustine, one of the greatest prodigals of them all, came to the same discovery. 'You have made us for yourself,' he confessed to God, 'and our hearts are restless till they find their rest in you.' We toy with material things, trying to slake a thirst that lies not in the physical realm but in the personal. That, of course, is why personal relationships are so important to us. The experience of human love points to an ultimate relationship. It reflects a greater destiny for which we were made, which is to be in fellowship with God. But no human relationship, no matter how deep, real and long-lasting, can ever really satisfy the hunger of our soul. We delude ourselves if we think it otherwise. It's simply one more route to disillusionment if we invest that kind of ultimate importance in a boyfriend, girlfriend or spouse. Such an expectation is bound to let us down, no matter how wonderful that other person is. No-one can sustain that weight of significance in our lives, for it's a weight only God can carry.

Jean-Paul Sartre, the French philosopher, was an atheist. How perfectly he spoke for modern men and women when he wrote, 'That God does not exist I cannot doubt, but that my whole being cries out for God I cannot deny.'

Sitting in his pigsty, the boy in the story appreciates his true identity as the son of his father. That's where he had gone wrong. He had tried to run away from that identity; he had sought an impossible freedom, failing to realize there are some freedoms that are simply not accessible to us because they contradict who we are. Jesus would have us reach the same conclusion. Our bid for moral autonomy is doomed to failure. We can't run away from God; the hole inside us will still be there – aching with a spiritual hunger only he can meet.

The first thing this boy has to face up to, then, is that he's lost. The second is that he is *guilty*. 'I will . . . go back . . . and say . . . : Father . . . I am no longer worthy to be called your son,' he says to himself. At this key point in the story Jesus is reminding us that the root of our folly is our moral decision to try to be independent of God. This is how we have got ourselves into our confused mess. We've flouted God's rules, and as a result we have offended and hurt him. 'We have sinned against heaven and against you,' to use the boy's words.

It's important we understand this. Some people think of God as some kind of cosmic traffic warden who's got a set of impersonal laws that he's duty bound to enforce, but with which he doesn't really feel personally involved. Jesus' story reveals that it is not like that at all. The moral law is the law of God's own heart and nature. When we sin, when we fail to love people as he says we should, when we fail to speak the truth as he tells us we should, when we fail to honour our parents as he says we should, and particularly when we fail to love him and honour him as he says we should, we are not simply parking on a heavenly double yellow line. Rather, we are parking on the traffic warden's foot! We are offending him personally. He feels angry and hurt about it.

If we have any doubt about this, then we must look at the cross. That stark symbol of agonized death is there to show us how much the sin of the world offends, angers and hurts God. It demonstrates how much it cost him personally to keep the door of reconciliation open to us. The boy had to realize not just that he was lost, but that he was guilty; not simply that he needed his father's fellowship, but that he needed his father's forgiveness. Once he discovered that, Jesus tells us, only a few short steps separated him from joy. But I think they must have been the hardest steps he ever took in his entire life.

> 'I will set out and go back to my father' (Luke 15:18).

A minister of a church once met a boy who had run away from home, and counselled him. He pointed to this very parable of the wasteful son, and advised: 'Now, you go back to your father and see if he doesn't kill the fatted calf to welcome you.'

Some weeks later he met the boy again on the street.

'Did you go back to your dad?' he asked.

'Yes, I did,' he replied.

'And did you apologize?'

'Yes, I did,' he nodded.

'And did he kill the fatted calf?'

'No,' said the boy, 'he jolly well near killed the prodigal son!'

By contrast, the warmth of the father's reception of this boy in Jesus' story is surprising. It's unlike most of us to be reconciled so totally, with no recriminations, no grievances.

> While [the son] was still a long way off, his father saw him and was filled with compassion for him; he ran to his son, threw his arms around him and kissed him (Luke 15:20).

It would have been so human for the father to have made the boy squirm a bit for his folly, to have demanded some restitution or inflicted some punishment. But the story has none of that. Instead we are presented with a wonderful readiness to forgive. The father seems to have been waiting and watching even while the boy's back was turned against him. Notice how the father *runs* to him? In the ancient world that was something a senior man simply would not do in public. It was considered undignified. Clearly this man's heart is so full that it compels him, careless of the embarrassment or of what his neighbours might think, to pick up his long gown and run! He is filled, says Jesus, with compassion for the boy. He throws his arms around him and, to translate the Greek a little more precisely, covers him with tender kisses.

The boy, for his part, has determined that he is going to try to make it up with his father. His thought is to offer to work as a wage labourer on the family farm, so as to repay the money he had so recklessly wasted. The father, however, will hear none of it. He does not even give him the opportunity to make such an offer. He interrupts the boy in mid-confession. 'Quick'! he orders his servants,

> Bring the best robe and put it on him. Put a ring on his finger and sandals on his feet. Bring the fattened calf and kill it. Let's have a feast and celebrate. For this son of mine was dead and is alive again; he was lost and is found (Luke 15:22–24).

Jesus the story-teller, then, is making a very wonderful point. If we have had a big row with God, and our relationship with him is in tatters as a result, matters can be set right again. If we will come back to him in genuine repentance, turning from our rebellion and our foolish independence, seeking his face again, he is not going to grind our faces into the dirt beneath his feet, as many a human father would do. No, God is not going to make us feel ashamed, or put us into bondage as punishment. Jesus teaches us here the reliability of God's grace and mercy. He will rejoice, and all heaven with him, to have us back again.

It is true that we have turned our backs on him. In a hundred ways we've told him to get lost. But no matter how big the row that has divided us, he wants to make it up, and he will do so. Even now he waits. He waits for sinners, people who know they're on the wrong side of him, to come back. When they do so he will not let them take the role of a slave. He invests in them the dignity of being his sons and his daughters.

But the story has not yet ended. There is a sting in the tail!

> Meanwhile, the older son was in the field (Luke 15:25).

Why does Jesus now introduce him? The answer lies in

remembering the original context of the story. This parable, we said, was not primarily designed as a therapeutic word of comfort to those sinners Jesus was eating with. It was a Stealth bomber charged with the mission of exploding the complacency of those so-called 'saints' who were criticizing him for eating with the 'sinners'. And it is those so-called 'saints' that this elder brother so clearly represents. This is evident from what he says about himself.

> *'Look! All these years I've been slaving for you and never disobeyed your orders'* (Luke 15:29).

There is the perfect son for you. Surely he has to be Jesus' ideal. For years he'd been serving his father, and had never rebelled. Or had he? Is there perhaps just a hint of petulance, of whining self-pity, in that phrase, 'All these years I've been slaving for you'? Are we wrong to detect the thinly veiled resentment of one who'd been 'working my fingers to the bone for you'? We know exactly what people mean when they talk like that. His do-gooding, you see, has no more liberated him as a personality than his brother's licentiousness had. Rather, it has rendered him humourless, prudish, constrained in his affections, incapable of enjoying himself, repressed, inhibited, pouting, and censorious. He condemns his brother, not because he really feels outraged by his brother's behaviour, but because he envies him. Listen to what he says about him: 'He has squandered your property with prostitutes' (Luke 15:30) – the unspoken grudge being, 'I would like to have done that, but I never did. And you've never rewarded me with a roast goat so that I could celebrate with my friends.' He's jealous of his brother – it is as simple as that.

There are hundreds of people like that today: respectable, conventional, good people. They look down their noses at the permissive society; they curl their lip at the decay in moral standards. They think they're good, but they are not; they're simply dull. They think they're being moral, but they are not; they're merely feeling sanctimonious. They think they are Christians, but they are not; they are Pharisees. Jesus would have us know how huge the difference is. Joyless in their hypocrisy, sterile in their respectability, their religion has no more in common with Christianity than a frigid marriage has in common with a real love affair.

The elder brother had fallen victim to the slow freeze. It is true that he was still at home, but his relationship with his father was as distant as his brother's in the remote country. Notice what Jesus says of him in verse 28: he 'refused to go in.' He chose to miss the party. His father threw a great celebration, and this elder brother had not got the grace to enjoy it. Instead, he makes a big public scene on the doorstep, with all the neighbours looking through their windows. The embarrassment of a middle-eastern father in such a situation is not hard to imagine. Yet his arms of mercy are open to this son just as they were open to the younger one. Notice how the father comes out to him, just as he went out to the prodigal. He pleads with him. Just as he showed compassion to his brother, so he encourages this son with tenderness and affection. 'My son,' he insists, 'everything I have is yours' (Luke 15:31). He tells him how precious he is to him, how appreciated and valued. Yet he still refuses to go in to the party.

Can anyone be so foolish as to choose hell in preference to heaven? Yes, they can! And the reason lies in a single word; pride. Pride is the thick hide that grace simply cannot penetrate. Think of that younger boy when he had been in the pigsty, coming to his senses, seeing what a fool he had been. He could have kept his pride and stayed in that pigsty had he wanted to. The reason he was rescued and reconciled was that he had the humility to repent.

Many people feel remorse over their life, kicking themselves and telling themselves what fools they have been. But that feeling will not take you to the Father. Remorse is simply wounded pride, a wallowing in self-pity. Repentance begins only when you get up and come to the Father. It was that willingness to humble himself and to enter the house that the elder brother lacked. It was his pride that kept him outside, just as it was their pride that would keep the Pharisees and teachers of the law Jesus encountered outside the kingdom of heaven. It was their pride that would consent to his death and nail him to the cross.

Some of us think of judgment as God sorting out the human race into those who are going to heaven and those who are going to hell. The ones he likes he sends to heaven, and those he doesn't he sends to hell. But that is not the picture Jesus gives in this story. He portrays rather a God who overflows with grace and generosity, opening his arms to all: elder brother, younger brother; saint or sinner. He makes no distinctions. If we stay out of heaven it is because *we* refuse to go in. It is because *we* are too proud to accept his grace. This elder brother felt he deserved a reward. 'All these years I've been slaving for you.' Jesus is emphatic: we cannot have heaven as a reward, only as a gift – a gift we are humble enough to receive, knowing we don't deserve it.

Maybe, like the younger brother, you've had a big row with God, and are in the distant country, or in the pigsty. Now that you have thought about it, you know that a lot of what Jesus is saying about the lost son is true of you. Is it pride that prevents you from coming back home?

Perhaps you are like the elder brother. You have grown up in a Christian home, maybe. You have a religious background. You are very morally minded. But as John Wesley said of the years before he became a Christian, 'I had then the religion of a servant, not of a son.' Is it pride in you that wants to earn your ticket to heaven, and hasn't yet learned to open your arms to God's generosity and say, 'Thank you'?

All of us would feel a lot more comfortable about the thought of becoming Christians if only we could walk into heaven with our heads held high, with everybody clapping and congratulating us. 'You made it! What an achievement! Well done, old chap!' But none of us can enter heaven in that way. There is only one way back to the Father, according to Jesus, and that is on our knees, humbly accepting his grace and mercy, like a son who was lost, and then was found again.

5

A long-term investment

Luke 16:19–31

'There was a rich man who dressed in purple and fine linen and lived in luxury every day. [20]At his gate was laid a beggar named Lazarus, covered with sores [21]and longing to eat what fell from the rich man's table. Even the dogs came and licked his sores.

[22]'The time came when the beggar died and the angels carried him to Abraham's side. The rich man also died and was buried. [23]In hell, where he was in torment, he looked up and saw Abraham far away, with Lazarus by his side. [24]So he called to him, "Father Abraham, have pity on me and send Lazarus to dip the tip of his finger in water and cool my tongue, because I am in agony in this fire."

[25]'But Abraham replied, "Son, remember that in your lifetime you received your good things, while Lazarus received bad things, but now he is comforted here and you are in agony. [26]And besides all this, between us and you a great chasm has been fixed, so that those who want to go from here to you cannot, nor can anyone cross over from there to us."

[27]'He answered, "Then I beg you, father, send Lazarus to my father's house, [28]for I have five brothers. Let him warn them, so that they will not also come to this place of torment."

[29]'Abraham replied, "They have Moses and the Prophets; let them listen to them."

[30]'"No, father Abraham," he said, "but if someone from the dead goes to them, they will repent."

[31]'He said to him, "If they do not listen to Moses and the Prophets, they will not be convinced even if someone rises from the dead." '

Few words have been bandied around more freely in the last hundred years or so than the word 'equality'. Class equality, race equality, sex equality – such concerns have dominated the political agenda. Aristocrats have been executed, politicians assassinated, and governments toppled, all in the name of equality. Indeed, so universal is the egalitarian dream, that it is ironic that the world should have been so long divided between the West and the East. For the American Constitution and the Communist Manifesto have the word 'equality' in common. One calls for equality of distribution in a cooperative society, the other for equality of opportunity in a competitive society. The one calls for fair *shares* for all, the other for a fair *chance* for all. But both are fundamentally agreed that justice is essentially about equality. That being so, I suppose there are few stories that Jesus ever told which have quite the same obvious degree of relevance to our twentieth-century social conscience as that of the rich man and Lazarus. Here surely is Jesus' comment on the problem of inequality in our human society.

It is the story of two men, two destinies and five brothers. Of the two men, the first was phenomenally wealthy. It is a sad thing when the only obituary a person can have is the bold statement that he was rich, but that's the only one Jesus can find for this fellow. He tells us that the man dressed expensively, wearing the best and most fashionable clothes money could buy – 'purple and fine linen'. He lived sumptuously, not a day passing without some splendid banquet being held. And his dwelling was ostentatious. This 'gate' that Jesus mentions was not the normal sort of gate that you and I might have on the side entrance of our house. It was a huge ornamental portico such as usually adorned palaces or temples. Material prosperity oozed out of every pore of this fellow, then – his clothes, his food, his house. 'He was rich' – but that is all we are told. Nothing about his friends, achievements, or even conspicuous vices – just 'rich' (Luke 16:19). Jesus' story implies that there is something very tragic about a person who can be summed up like that.

The second man could not have been more different.

> *At his gate was laid a beggar named Lazarus, covered with sores and longing to eat what fell from the rich man's table* (Luke 16:20–21).

So Jesus paints a picture of abject poverty as extreme as the rich man's opulence. He was *'laid* at his gate', he says. But this is too gentle a translation. The original literally says that he was *thrown* at his gate. As we might say, he was *sprawled* there to face the sneering contempt of passers-by. He had no fine clothes. The only things that covered his back were untreated sores; some skin disease, probably, resulting from chronic malnutrition. For he was permanently hungry. The mere sight of the garbage from the rich man's banquet brought saliva foaming to his mouth. But the only real compassion he experienced was shown by the mangy mongrels of the streets. 'Even the dogs . . . licked his sores' (Luke 16:21). Notice the stress on that word *even*. Just as in the tale of the lost son in the last chapter, Jesus uses the companionship of animals to emphasize how low this fellow had got. Almost dehumanized, his human dignity was trampled upon and disgraced.

There was one thing, however, that this poor man had which the rich man did not. Something so common its profundity is easily missed. This poor man had a *name*, Lazarus. It is most unusual for Jesus to give the characters in his stories names. In fact, this is the only occasion he does. So odd is it that some have been tempted to argue that this is a factual incident that Jesus is relating, and not a story at all. But there are no real grounds for claiming that. No, Jesus gives this poor man a name because in the context of his story the name is significant. It is there for a reason. You see, you need a name only if you are known to somebody. A name is an instrument of personal relationship. To know somebody's name is to distinguish that precious individual out of the seething mass of the crowd.

To have a name is to be a person, to be valuable, to be significant, to matter to somebody. The rich man had no name. This does not mean that there was a blank on his birth certificate. Indeed, in the daily newspapers of his day, I expect that he was 'well known'. The point is, however, that as far as Jesus' story is concerned, his name is irrelevant. For he was just rich, nothing else. He spent his money on material luxury. Other *people* didn't feature on his agenda. And as a result he didn't feature on theirs. He didn't need a name; he was just a faceless millionaire. That was his tragedy.

The poor man, however, was not anonymous. Somebody knew him personally, and Jesus gives us the name Lazarus to tell us who that somebody was. In the Hebrew, Lazarus is Eleazar, and it means 'he whom God helps.' It was God, then, who cared for this man. A pauper like him might have plotted revenge or harboured bitterness. He might have blamed his misfortune on God, and cursed him for his misery. But by giving him the name Lazarus, Jesus is indicating that this poor man did none of these things. By his patience and faith he proved himself to be the man who looks to God alone for his vindication. He was one whom God helps, a man in whom trials have bred not resentment, or self-pity, but faith.

Here then are two totally unequal men – the one with wealth but no identity, and the other utterly poor, yet known personally to God. Ask yourself, which would you rather have been? There is, you see, such a thing as spiritual as well as material inequality. And the purpose of this story is to warn us that very often they are inversely proportional to each other. 'Blessed are the poor in spirit,' Jesus said, 'for theirs is the kingdom of heaven' (Matthew 5:3). 'What good is it for a man to gain the whole world, and yet lose or forfeit his very self?' (Luke 9:25).

That brings us to the second aspect of the story. The two men have two very different destinies.

> *The time came when the beggar died and the angels carried him to Abraham's side. The rich man also died and was buried. In hell, where he was in torment, he looked up and saw Abraham far away, with Lazarus by his side. So he called to him, 'Father Abraham, have pity on me and send Lazarus to dip the tip of his finger in water and cool my tongue, because I am in agony in this fire'* (Luke 16:22–24).

We have to be very careful how we interpret the horrifying elements of these particular verses.

First of all, this is a parable, and a parable is a literary device for teaching spiritual truths by allegorical means. Parables, therefore, are not meant to be read like history. Even more important, as far as this particular parable is concerned, Jesus is quite clearly here accommodating himself to the conventional Jewish ideas of that period about the afterlife. I don't think there can be any other explanation for his strange description of going to heaven as being carried by the angels to Abraham's side. That's a metaphor without parallel in the rest of the New Testament, but it's common enough in the rabbinical writings of Jesus' own day. In fact, scholars have discovered a story quite similar to this one. It probably originated in Egypt, and was very popular among Jews in Palestine in the first century. It is far from impossible that Jesus is deliberately using that common folk tale in order to make a point of his own here.

For both of these reasons, therefore, it would be unwise to press the details of this account of the afterlife too far. Some, for instance, have questioned whether Jesus is describing here some intermediate state, in which the soul survives after death before the general resurrection. The implication of the story certainly seems to be that life is continuing as normal on planet Earth while the rich man and Lazarus enter their experience of the afterlife. Yet if they are disembodied souls, why does Jesus speak as if they had physical bodies? He mentions the rich man's tongue and Lazarus' finger. At the very least, we have to say there is a high degree of probability that Jesus' language here is symbolic, and that we had better not read it as if it were a literal account of what the afterlife is like.

Having entered that cautionary note, however, it is very hard to imagine Jesus casting his story in this form, or even repeating an existing story like this, if he didn't intend to endorse, at least in outline, the picture it gives us of human destiny. Indeed, the story falls apart if certain aspects of it are not an accurate picture of the afterlife. Maybe he isn't intending to detail the real nature of heaven and hell to us. But it is surely his intention to warn us that heaven and hell exist. He surely suggests that our personalities survive death in a conscious state. He certainly implies that a distinction between human beings occurs at death. The personalities of the dead are sustained by God in two quite different states: the one a state of bliss, in company with the redeemed of every age (represented by Abraham); the other a state of isolated anguish, represented by the lonely rich man in hell. If these things are not true in outline, then the whole point of Jesus' story is lost.

And that of course is a very sobering observation. People sometimes remark that death is the great equalizer. No matter how great or wealthy you may have been in this life, no matter how high you may rise over the heads of your fellows, there's no evading that final horizontal repose by which all people are reduced to a common level. Remember the famous words of Thomas Gray's *Elegy*:

The boast of heraldry, the pomp of pow'r,
    And all that beauty, all that wealth e'er gave,
Awaits alike th'inevitable hour,
    The paths of glory lead but to the grave.

It is true, of course, that death recognizes no class distinctions; it mocks them by its grim indiscrimination. Yet this story does not speak of death as equalizing people's fortunes. It portrays rather a great reversal of fortune. Society beyond the grave, according to Jesus, is no more egalitarian than this one is. It is riven, he says, by a barrier a thousand times more polarized and uncrossable than any social distinction this world has ever known. Notice how Abraham puts it in the story:

> 'Besides all this, between us and you a great chasm
> has been fixed, so that those who want to go from
> here to you cannot, nor can anyone cross over from
> there to us' (Luke 16:26).

What was it about the rich man that merited such an appalling judgment – that his destiny was fixed in that awful place for eternity, with no way out? What was it that could possibly have deserved such a fate? What had he done wrong?

We need to be careful in analysing why the fates of the rich man and the poor man were so different. Some, I suspect, will be tempted to read into this story some kind of quasi-Marxist critique of economic disparity in society. Lazarus going to heaven, and the rich man to hell, is a spiritualization of the victory of the working classes over the exploitative bourgeoisie. Such an interpretation would be very appealing to many, but it is quite out of step with the Bible, and would be totally unjustified from this story itself.

There is not a hint in this story, for instance, that wealth *per se* is immoral. Jesus is not suggesting that heaven exercises some kind of positive class discrimination towards the poor. Indeed, there's one element of this story that proves that beyond doubt – the presence of Abraham in heaven. No-one could ever represent Abraham as a representative of the down-trodden proletariat. The Bible makes it quite clear that the patriarch was fabulously wealthy by the end of his life; a very powerful, rich man. Abraham in heaven rules out any kind of naïve, Robin Hood idea, then, that all rich people are bad and all the poor are good. Jesus in this story does not suggest that the rich man got his money by improper means. There is no suggestion that he exploited or defrauded people. He may have got his wealth from his parents. If so, Jesus voices no complaint about the perpetuation of class privilege through the laws of inheritance. He might have earned his wealth in the market-place. If so, Jesus issues no denunciation of the capitalist system. The reason the rich man merited judgment must lie elsewhere. Jesus can't be saying that because he was rich he had to go to hell, or Abraham would be there too.

Now a good rule when you've got a problem in understanding the Bible is to examine more closely the context of the passage. When you do that, you discover that the section of chapter 16 before our story is in fact devoted to the subject of wealth. Jesus stresses there how important it is that we treat wealth as a trust, something we're responsible for using wisely. He says:

> If you have not been trustworthy in handling worldly wealth, who will trust you with true riches? And if you have not been trustworthy with someone else's property, who will give you property of your own? (Luke 16:11–12).

The true treasure of heaven, Jesus argues, is going to be given only to people who make proper use of their worldly treasure.

To explain what a 'proper use' is, Jesus actually told another story. It's quite an amusing one. It tells of a manager of a company who is dismissed by the owner of the company for wasting resources. Having been given his notice, the manager decides that with unemployment looming on the horizon he could do with a few friends. So he writes around to all the people who owe money to the company and tells them that he will settle their bills for half what they owe. When the owner discovered what he had done, Jesus says he had the good humour to congratulate the manager – not of course for his dishonesty, but for his shrewdness. Jesus draws this lesson:

> Use worldly wealth to gain friends for yourselves, so that when it is gone, you will be welcomed [or they will welcome you] into eternal dwellings (Luke 16:9).

Jesus' point seems to be that the manager had used the influence he had in regard to material things to bring blessing to other people, so that when that influence had gone, he had plenty of friends to speak for him and look after him. In the same way, says Jesus, make friends for yourself by the way you use your money, so that when material things fail, those friends will welcome *you* into heaven. Jesus isn't arguing for distributive justice of the Marxist kind, then. He's arguing for a concept of wealth which is largely ignored today – the concept of stewardship. Wealth, Jesus teaches, is a trust from God to be used not for yourself, but for the benefit of other people. If you want to invest in eternity, the only thing you can invest in is people. For people last, but money does not.

Luke tells us there were some Pharisees listening in to this story of the shrewd manager. They did not like what Jesus was saying, and for obvious reasons. They loved money. And Jesus' response is to launch one of his Stealth bombers again. This story of the rich man and Lazarus is told with his eye on those Pharisees. Beware, he's warning them, you can't serve God and money. Show me a man or woman dedicated to material acquisitiveness, claims Jesus, and I'll show you a hell-bound pagan. No matter how respectable they appear on the surface, or how regularly they attend church, or how well-thumbed is their Bible, they cannot serve two masters. They are going to be devoted either to the one or to the other. If you're devoted to money, by definition you hold God in contempt. Their love of money proved that the Pharisees' hearts were not with God, and that therefore their destiny could not be with God.

Our story then is a cautionary tale designed by Jesus to demonstrate the peril of a life dedicated to acquisitiveness. The rich man had every opportunity to lay up treasure in heaven by investing his material resources in this poor man and thus making him his friend. He then would have been using his wealth as a wise steward for the benefit of others rather than for his own self-indulgence. But he conspicuously failed to do so. His condemnation was not a verdict on the way he became wealthy, or on the fact that he was wealthy. His tragedy was that he was *just* wealthy. There was nothing else to write in his obituary. He committed no murder, no adultery, no theft. If you had accused him in the street he would have shrugged his shoulders indignantly and said, 'I've done nothing wrong,' and it would be true in a sense. For it was not for the bad things that he had done, but for the good things he had left undone, that this man went to hell. You had your good things, says Abraham, but the beggar at your gate never benefited from them. You had the opportunity to use your wealth to help him and you refused. That's why you are there, rich man. Money mattered more to you than people. Heaven would be hell for a person like you!

Often we take refuge in our negative righteousness – all

those 'thou shalt nots' that we have so carefully observed. Jesus here expresses the hollow mockery of the goodness which such negative righteousness represents. Sins of omission, he says, are just as damning as sins of commission. 'Whatever you did not do for one of the least of these, you did not do for me' (Matthew 25:45).

Notice the irony of the rich man's words in hell: 'Send Lazarus . . .' This self-sufficient man had never before needed anybody, least of all that beggar at his gate. What use was a beggar to him? Now suddenly he needs someone; and of all people, he needs Lazarus. But now there is nobody to satisfy his need. His independence of others has been hardened into a fixed and unchangeable isolation.

Sometimes I've heard people say that they wouldn't mind being in hell. They would have plenty of their mates to keep them company. Where were the rich man's mates? Such isolation is the pathos of hell. T. S. Eliot wrote: 'Hell is oneself, Hell is alone.' Hell is the agony of being unable to love or be loved. Hell is the realization of one's need of others, but a need that can no longer be met and which leaves us only with the regret of lost opportunity. Notice too Abraham's charge to the rich man to 'remember'. Once, the gap between him and Lazarus had not been insuperable; a channel of communication had been available between them at one time. But things have changed now. A great void had been fixed by the decree of God. All that was left, therefore, was the tormenting knowledge of the opportunity he had forfeited. Sometimes you hear people talk about purgatory as a place where we can atone for our sins, and then win a second chance. Jesus doesn't seem to give any such hope here. This great chasm of which Abraham speaks is the end of chances. We are on probation here and now; we are sealing our destinies here and now.

Notice, further, that Abraham replies to the rich man as 'son'. There's something very tender about that, but also significant. This man was a son of Abraham; a Jew, in other words; a member of God's covenant people, at least by birth. He was a son of Abraham, and yet in hell. This was unthinkable to the Jews then and perhaps unthinkable for some of us today. How can God send me to hell? I'm a Christian; I'm a church-goer; I've got a Christian Union membership card. We need to heed the warning of Jesus. The fire and physical torture may be symbols, but they symbolize something real, dreadful and final. Most disturbing of all, they symbolize something which a person can slide into by no more than a sin of negligence, while being a so-called Christian all the time.

How can I test whether my Christianity is the genuine article or not? According to Jesus in this story, one criterion is to ask what use I am making of my material resources. If I belong to God, then so does my money. I will see myself as a steward of what I have. I will see myself as entrusted with what I have, and will desire to use it in a way that will please God. If our hearts are not God's, then we will view ourselves as owners, and use what we have without reference to him or the values he represents.

This is where the five brothers come in. The rich man pleads:

> 'I beg you, father, send Lazarus to my father's house, for I have five brothers. Let him warn them, so that they will not also come to this place of torment' (Luke 16:27–28).

So the Stealth bomber drops its load. Up to this point Jesus' audience would not perhaps have been greatly surprised by the story. The familiar tale from Egypt had a similar kind of ironic reversal in the afterlife too. But this closing part of the story is unique to Jesus. Here is the sting in the tail, typically incisive. The five brothers of course are you and me, the Pharisees in his audience, or indeed anybody else listening to the story. The destiny of Lazarus and the rich man is now determined, but not that of the five brothers, and not ours. We are still here, and have opportunity. The rich man would like to send us a ghostly emissary to warn us of the reality of the life to come. Like Dickens in *A Christmas Carol*, he is sure that a suitable apparition will work a conversion on our Scrooge-like hearts. Notice heaven's verdict on such a stratagem:

> Abraham replied, 'They have Moses and the Prophets; let them listen to them.'
> 'No, father Abraham . . . if someone from the dead goes to them, they will repent.'
> He said to him, 'If they do not listen to Moses and the Prophets, they will not be convinced even if someone rises from the dead' (Luke 16:29–31).

Jesus' story of the rich man and Lazarus teaches some very sobering lessons: the dangers of using wealth selfishly, the seriousness of sins of omission, and the reality of heaven and hell. But the last, I suggest, is the most crucial lesson of all. What turns a person's heart from selfishness, greed, complacency and indifference to the love of God? What works repentance and faith in a person's heart and puts him or her on the pathway to heaven? Some people answer that spiritualism can do it. Going along to a séance, and meeting your departed relative, imparts a certainty about the afterlife. Others believe that signs and wonders are the answer. Perform a few healings in church on Sunday night, and people will be clamouring to become Christians.

Jesus' claim is rather the reverse. He insists that even if someone rose from the dead, it would not guarantee the conversion of the world. There's only one thing, he argues, that has the power actually to create faith and repentance in a person's life. Perhaps unexpectedly, he says it is the Bible. If people won't listen to 'Moses and the Prophets', nothing else will work, not even somebody rising from the dead. And he should know, of course, because he did!

Jesus tells us, then, that we seal our destiny by our response to the Bible. Signs and wonders may establish the faith of the faithful, and may confirm the spiritual blindness of the unbelieving. But it is the Word of God that awakens spiritual life.

Every time we open God's book, we stand before the gates of heaven and hell. That is the measure of how serious it is to hear the Word of God. It is not like reading a novel. For this is a word that calls us to change. No ghost is going to warn you of judgment to come. No miracle is going to prove to you the power of unseen things. Like the five brothers, you can have an open Bible in front of you; that is your privilege.

Not all the world has that privilege, I freely acknowledge. For some, the Bible is still an unknown book. What Jesus would say of those more remote brothers of the rich man, we don't know for sure. Perhaps he would say that they have the book of nature and the light of conscience. The point is, however, that this is not addressed to people like that; it is addressed to people like us who have a Bible.

And what Jesus is saying to us on that score is quite simple. If we will not listen to the Bible we will listen to nothing. If we will not be changed by it we will be changed by nothing.

Perhaps Jesus is rather more realistic about the question of equality than our modern world tends to be. People today speak of equality of wealth in places where there never has been equality of wealth, and I doubt whether there ever will be. Jesus once commented, 'You will always have the poor among you' (John 12:8). Equality of opportunity is also elusive, I'm afraid, if you press it too far. People are born with a huge variety of potential; as

Jesus himself put it, to one five talents, to another two, to another one. But does it matter? In Jesus' mind, wealth and opportunity are gifts within the providence of God. We don't own them, but are entrusted with them. It is what we do with that trust, the opportunity or the wealth that we are given, that determines the spiritual calibre and spiritual direction of our hearts. Five brothers: some rich, some poor, some able, some incompetent, some lucky and some unlucky. But all of them equally responsible to heed the warning of the Book and choose the way that goes to heaven.

6

The paradox of pardon

Luke 18:9–14

To some who were confident of their own righteousness and looked down on everybody else, Jesus told this parable: [10]*"Two men went up to the temple to pray, one a Pharisee and the other a tax collector.* [11]*The Pharisee stood up and prayed about himself: "God, I thank you that I am not like other men – robbers, evildoers, adulterers – or even like this tax collector.* [12]*I fast twice a week and give a tenth of all I get."*

[13]*'But the tax collector stood at a distance. He would not even look up to heaven, but beat his breast and said, "God, have mercy on me, a sinner."*

[14]*'I tell you that this man, rather than the other, went home justified before God. For everyone who exalts himself will be humbled, and he who humbles himself will be exalted.'*

Jack and Joe went to church one evening. Jack knew his way around. Well, he'd been brought up in the place, hadn't he? Sunday School from the age of three, and all that. He knew his parents would be there, too, in one of the other pews, watching him proudly. He wanted to make sure they saw him. So he walked right up to the front and sat in the first row. He bowed his head and shut his eyes for a few moments. He'd seen dad do that; he knew it looked holy.

Jack, you see, took his religion very seriously. He carried a big Bible and knew all the latest choruses. He liked the image of being a highly principled young man, too. Unlike many of his peers he never consumed alcohol or cigarettes. He was also extremely self-righteous about sex. No messing around behind the school bike sheds for him. He and his girlfriend had intellectual conversations about vegetarianism and the nuclear issue. Instead of going to discos they went to prayer meetings at the youth leader's house.

As Jack reflected on his life in those few moments before the service began, he glowed with inward satisfaction. How reassuring it was to know that you were a good Christian! Nothing to confess, nothing to feel ashamed about, nothing . . .

Good grief, it couldn't be! Out of the corner of his eye he caught sight of a familiar figure who had just entered the church behind him. 'It's Joe,' he thought incredulously. 'What on earth is he doing here? He's no right to come to church, the old hypocrite!' But if he had been able to read Joe's mind he would have realized that precisely the same thoughts were going through his head too.

What right, Joe thought, did he have to be in church? He hadn't been in church for years. In fact he felt thoroughly uncomfortable in the place. He kept looking around nervously as if he expected somebody in authority to appear at any moment and tell him he had no business to be there. He was unsure where to sit, or if there was some special ritual he should observe before committing himself to stay. Didn't Christians cross themselves before they sat down in church? Or was that Muslim? He really couldn't remember. In the end he slid cautiously into the very back row. 'Oh no,' he wailed inwardly, 'that's Jack in the front, and he's seen me. I'll never live this down in the neighbourhood now.' He crumpled up, his legs tucked under the pew, his head sagging down between his knees, trying to hide.

As you may have guessed, Joe was not the religious sort. In fact he had a reputation as a bit of a lad. If there was trouble with the police on the estate, you could bet on the fact that he'd be involved. Nicotine stained his fingers and there was a distinct smell of beer on his breath. In fact he'd been in the pub down the road only fifteen minutes before.

Why on earth had he come to church? Was it because of the row he'd had that morning at home, thrown out on his ear for stealing his mother's housekeeping again? Or was it because of the sense of humiliation he was feeling as a result of Julie slapping him around the face last night and telling him in unambiguous four-letter words to get out of her life, just because she discovered he was also sleeping with Karen? Yes, it was both of those things and neither of them. Somehow, as he tried unsuccessfully to drown his sorrows in that pint, he'd just been overcome with a sense of how dirty he was, and what a mess he'd made of things. Suddenly, sitting in that back pew, guilt and shame brought tears to his eyes, a blush to his cheek and a lump to his throat. 'Oh, God,' he sighed quietly, into clenched fists. 'Oh, God.'

I tell you, it was Joe who went home a believer that night, not Jack.

For everyone who exalts himself will be humbled, and he who humbles himself will be exalted (Luke 18:14).

We said earlier that one of the great problems in reading the parables today is the difficulty of recovering the shock factor that they undoubtedly possessed for Jesus' original hearers. Too often, familiarity with these stories has disarmed them of their punch for us, deprived us of the sting in the tale.

Take the story of the good Samaritan which we studied in chapter 2. The very word 'Samaritan' has become proverbial for goodness. So when Jesus tells us that it was a Samaritan who stopped to help the injured man, we're not surprised, still less outraged. There's no scandalized intake of breath at the mere mention of the word, as there certainly would have been when the parable was first told. The hammer-blows the parable delivered to the prejudices of Jesus' original audience are reduced, for us, to the caress of a reassuring feather. We know all about good Samaritans.

Even more is that true of the parable to which we turn in this chapter. I have retold it in modern dress in an attempt to help us feel more powerfully the contradiction of conventional expectation that it represents.

Think about it for a moment. Two men went up to the temple to pray. A self-evidently laudable ambition, you would have thought. Both came to pray and both went home believing sincerely that they had prayed. Yet the extraordinary lesson of this parable is that while one of them truly did have dealings with God in his devotions that day, the other, in spite of his avowed good intentions, was conducting a soliloquy all the time he was in the temple.

The text which our translation renders 'prayed about himself' (verse 11) could equally be translated, 'prayed *to* himself'. The prayer was indeed a soliloquy. That alone should be sufficient to worry us, shouldn't it? Yet Jesus says it is possible to come to church thinking that you want to meet with God, and leave believing you have done so, and all the time be self-deceived. What a disturbing challenge to the reality of our own spiritual experience that must be!

But the paradox is even sharper than that. And it's here that the modern reader so easily forfeits the scandalous element in the story. For Jesus tells us that the man whose prayer was heard was a tax man. For us, that occasions no surprise. In our society, representatives of the Inland Revenue, generally speaking, are pillars of the Establishment; we make occasional sarcastic jokes about them, but none of us would question their respectability.

Not so this tax man. In Jesus' day a tax man was a crook, a treacherous, despicable collaborator with the Roman enemy, who made himself rich by exploiting his fellow countrymen. Think of some provincial mayor in France lining his fat pockets during the days of the

Occupation by licking the boots of the Nazis, and you get the feel of how Jews felt about tax men in the first century. They didn't make sarcastic jokes about tax men, they lynched them. They spat on them when they passed and cursed the ground they walked on. Yet God heard the *tax man's* prayer – the very person they would never have listened to, let alone helped, in a thousand years.

On the other hand, the man who went home unheard, Jesus tells us, was a Pharisee. Once again, as modern readers we so easily miss the outrage of such a suggestion. For if we know from childhood that Samaritans are proverbially good, then even more do we know from childhood that Pharisees are proverbially bad. As soon as Jesus identifies this man as a Pharisee, we conclude that he's going to be the villain of the piece. All kinds of negative and damning associations flow into our minds at the mere mention of the word 'Pharisee'.

Once again, that would not have been the reaction of Jesus' original hearers. For the Pharisee was the churchman, the Bible student; fundamentalist in his view of Scripture, scrupulous in his observance of God's law, a patriot, a philanthropist, a model of holiness, an enthusiastic supporter of Mary Whitehouse, 'Keep Sunday Special' and the Moral Majority.

This is one parable the shock factor of which we just can't afford to miss. Jesus has got something vital to teach us here about the whole nature of religion, of prayer, of guilt, of righteousness; and we dare not allow our twentieth-century images of tax men and Pharisees to blunt the force of his warnings.

So try hard with me to get under the surface of this parable into the shoes of Jesus' original hearers, and benefit from it.

First, let's ask a question. What was so wrong with the Pharisee's prayer and right about the tax man's prayer, that God's assessment of them should be so radically different from our expectations? I don't think the answer is difficult to spot. Notice how the Pharisee begins. 'Lord,' he says, 'I thank you that I am not like other men.'

Can you imagine a man going to his doctor and saying, 'Doctor, I want you to know that I am in superb health; my lungs are functioning perfectly, my muscle tone is ideal, my digestion couldn't be better, my circulation is A1, I have no infections, no ailments, no diseases. In short, Doctor, unlike the rest of the miserable specimens I observe in your waiting-room, there's absolutely nothing wrong with me at all.'

What could a doctor do for such a man? He would leave the surgery unchanged, unbenefited in any way. There's little point in visiting at all, except to parade as a kind of one-man medical beauty show. He could receive nothing, because he asked for nothing. And why does he ask for nothing? Because he feels no need.

Had he allowed the doctor to examine him, his confidence may have been rather diminished. 'Your blood pressure's a bit high,' the doctor might have said. 'And we must do some tests on that mysterious lump, and I would let the dentist have a look at that tooth if I were you. And did you know you were diabetic?'

But such is the man's complacency, he never invites such an examination. The absence of any felt need renders his attendance at the doctor's clinic totally redundant.

That is exactly the point Jesus makes in another saying: 'It is not the healthy who need a doctor, but the sick' (Matthew 9:12). This Pharisee is a perfect example of that observation. He came into the temple to congratulate himself on his spiritual and moral health. Augustine wisely comments on him, 'Thou hast said thou hast all; thou hast asked for nothing. In what respect then hast thou come to pray?' He hadn't come to pray at all, but to prate. It was all exhibitionist boasting and nothing more.

I suspect that the tax man knew for whose benefit the Pharisee's 'prayer' was really intended. He overheard him, of course; how could he help it? 'God, I thank you', said the Pharisee loudly, 'that I'm not like other men, rogues, swindlers, traitors, or like that tax man over there.' It was a deliberate dig at him. But then he was used to such abuse. He didn't resent it; why should he? He knew he deserved it, he was under no illusions about his moral and spiritual condition, he was painfully aware of the disease of his soul. There was a mark of judgment set against his destiny, he knew.

And for this reason we hear no self-congratulatory expressions of mock gratitude from his lips. He feels his need. He beats his breast with the sense of it – a gesture no Jew made except in times of profound emotional distress. It bursts out of him in three staccato gasps of inner torture. 'God, be merciful to *me, the sinner.*' That's what he says literally; '*the* sinner', for at this moment he feels like the only sinner in the universe. Yet, says Jesus, that's the kind of prayer God hears. That sort of worshipper goes home a different person, whereas the proud and complacent, for all their eloquent supplications, leave the house of God in exactly the same unacceptable state in which they arrived. One recalls Mary's words: 'He has filled the hungry with good things but has sent the rich away empty' (Luke 1:53).

This question of personal felt need may very well be the crunch issue for many. How hungry are we for God? How desperate are we for his grace?

Much has been said in recent years about the renewal of worship in the church; in fact it made the headlines when the present Archbishop of Canterbury was enthroned. But it does seem to me that much of that controversy is concerned with things of interest to the Pharisee but not to the tax man. It's preoccupied with matters of external form. What type of music – traditional hymns or modern choruses? What sort of atmosphere – quiet and meditative or loud and excited? What kind of congregational participation – passive and restrained or active and exuberant? What degree of predictability –

fixed prayer-book liturgy or extemporary charismatic spontaneity? These are the issues we discuss. Frankly, while that sort of debate may well signal major changes in worship style, I'm not at all convinced that it has anything to do with renewal of worship in the spiritual sense at all.

Charles M. Schulz, the *Peanuts* cartoonist, suggested thirty years ago that most people attending church on Sunday do so with the same feelings as they attend the theatre; simply to enjoy what's going on. And he was absolutely right, in my view. The only thing he didn't take note of is that there are different kinds of entertainment, and how you express your enjoyment depends on the nature of the event. Schulz is quite right that some people come to church to sit passively listening as if at the theatre. But there are others who come with the same attitude with which they would attend a football match. And there are others who come with the same attitude with which they would attend a disco. With whatever attitude they come, however, they all come to enjoy what's going on. The worship style in which the church engages is no ground at all on which to judge the spirituality of those who are participating. Indeed, those of us who have travelled know that worship style is largely culturally determined. You go to a black Baptist church in the southern states of the USA and then to a Free Presbyterian in the Scottish Highlands and compare the difference! But the difference has nothing whatever to do with the spiritual authenticity of the worshippers. It's a cultural difference.

What determines whether we have real dealings with God when we go into his house to pray is not the music or the atmosphere, or even the degree of our physical participation in it. To think of worship in such terms is to think like a Judaistic Pharisee and not like a Christian at all. It is the hallmark of new-covenant religion that it is indifferent to cultural forms. 'A time is coming and has now come', said Jesus, 'when the true worshippers will worship the Father in spirit and truth, for they are the kind of worshippers the Father seeks' (John 4:23).

You want to know why that tax man was heard? It was because he had a heart for God. He felt the need for God. Worship for him was a matter of spirit and truth. That's why he went to church; not to be entertained, or, like the Pharisee, to entertain others. He went there as a sick man goes to a doctor, because he felt a profound personal moral desperation. God always hears the prayers of people like that, whoever they are: crooks, rogues, adulterers. Why, he even heard the eleventh-hour appeal of a thief on a cross. But he ignores, he snubs, those who come to his house as if they were attending a circus, simply to enjoy what's going on. After all, it's not as though they come to meet *him*, is it?

We will never have real dealings with God until we get beyond religious entertainment, until we reach this point of felt need which the tax man had reached. Then we will pray and get answers.

That brings us to the second thing Jesus highlights for us in this paradoxical little story: *two kinds of guilt*. The more you think about it, the more ironic it is: there was the tax man *feeling* guilty, yet Jesus says he went home acquitted; and there's the Pharisee *feeling* innocent, and Jesus implies he went home condemned. That pinpoints for us a very important distinction, between guilt as an emotional experience and guilt as an objective fact. And this little story points out that the presence or absence of the former doesn't necessarily imply the presence or absence of the latter.

We all know that there is such a thing as irrational guilt, guilt which feels out of proportion to any wrong we've actually committed. Psychiatrists have to deal with that kind of anxiety all the time. But what many people forget today is that it is equally possible to feel no guilt at all when in fact we should feel guilty. A complacent conscience may be psychologically innocuous. It may reduce our stress levels. I'm sure the Pharisee was far more relaxed and at ease with himself than this tax man was. And yet in ultimate spiritual terms, such a complacent conscience is dreadfully perilous.

For there is such a thing as real guilt. Guilt isn't just a feeling; it is a fact. Unfortunately the feeling and the fact don't always run together. In our increasingly psychologically aware generation we must not allow that objective reality of guilt to become obscured.

Some years ago I had a discussion with some GCSE English students who were studying Shakespeare's *Macbeth*. We were discussing the scene where Lady Macbeth, after the murder, is racked with anxiety about the image of blood which she sees indelibly clinging to her hands. What struck me was that their reaction was almost unanimous: not 'Here is a vicious criminal dreadfully convicted of her sin, who badly needs to find a sense of forgiveness,' but 'Here is a pathetic nutcase, seriously mentally disturbed, badly in need of a psychiatrist.'

Guilt has ceased to be an acceptable part of normal human experience in the twentieth century. It has become pathological. It's a symptom of emotional illness or mental abnormality now, rather than an appropriate moral response to personal sin. No longer do we send the guilt-stricken individual to the priest for absolution as we once did; we send them to the psychiatrist for treatment. And increasingly people think of the church itself as nothing more than an alternative form of such treatment. They go to church in order to feel better about themselves, in order to feel that they are OK people.

That, I suggest to you, was precisely the function of the Pharisee's piety. His religion was just a form of psychotherapy by which he got rid of his guilt feelings. Notice the three very obvious techniques he uses.

First, *he majors on negative obedience*. I commented on this in relation to the behaviour of the priest and the

Levite in the story of the good Samaritan. Here it is again. Our Pharisee comforts himself with all the sins he had *not* committed, like robbery or adultery. This is always good for the peace of our conscience, because of course such negative obedience forms a convenient smokescreen behind which we may conceal the many sins we *have* committed.

It's the kind of attitude which, as we said in our second study, lies behind a great deal of evasion of social responsibility today. It enables people to see a murder committed on a city street and do nothing about it, because they aren't personally holding the knife.

It's also the reason, incidentally, that religion has such a killjoy image in many people's minds. All those 'thou shalt nots'. Many think of God as a prohibitive spoilsport who wants to stop us doing all the things we want to do. Joy Davidman tells a lovely story of a missionary trying to convert an African chief. On being told that a long list of sins were indeed prohibited by Christian morality, he remarked that he was much too old to commit any of them anyway. 'So to be old and a Christian, they are the same thing!'

For many, that is exactly what being a Christian is: being old, being past it, giving oneself to God when the devil wants nothing more to do with us. They picture Christianity as something sapless and joyless, the enemy of all delights. And they think that way because so many religious people are trying to escape guilt by defining obedience in purely negative terms.

Secondly, *he majors on legalistic obedience*. He lists all the unnecessary good works of supererogation which he doesn't really have to do at all. Like fasting twice a week, when Moses said once a year was quite enough; or giving a tithe of absolutely everything he had – even the herbs in the kitchen which he used for flavouring his food – when Moses said a tithe of one's income was adequate.

Once again, legalism of this type is a classic method of

guilt avoidance. By accumulating a record of this kind of superfluous piety you can deceive yourself into thinking that you're compensating for any real sins that you may have committed. It's quite illogical, of course. You can never really make up for anything by subsequent penances of this sort. It's like going to the magistrate and saying, 'Yes, I did drive at 100 mph down the High Street yesterday. But unlike some people I never park on a double yellow line. Surely you can take that into consideration.'

Yet there are thousands of religious people whose minds work essentially in that fallacious fashion, pre-occupied with the trivial details of their lives in a desperate attempt to camouflage, and compensate for, a formidable monster of moral corruption that they know secretly lurks within. Some men take great pride in the fact that they don't smoke or drink, others are perfectionists in their hobbies, or workaholics in their careers. Some women are fanatically houseproud. They try to purge their conscience by liberal use of disinfectant in the bathroom. And of course there are those endless numbers of religious people who salve their consciences by attending church, giving money to charity, saying prayers, and so on. There's a certain kind of obsessive personality that enjoys ritual, discipline, self-denial, and that sort of thing. An ascetic, puritanical lifestyle is a form of self-indulgence for them.

And that's what the Pharisees were like. All such behaviour is driven by the desire to avoid guilt. By concentrating on the observance of petty rules and regulations which we set ourselves – rules which, though irksome, we know we can fully keep if we really try – our attention is diverted from God's big rules, with regard to which our obedience can never be satisfactory and which therefore provide us with an inexhaustible source of potential moral anxiety.

Third, *he majors on comparative obedience*. 'I am not', the

Pharisee says, 'like other men, that tax man for instance.' This strategy of self-justification never fails, for there are always people more guilty than ourselves. That is why we read the gutter press: to feed our own smug self-satisfaction. 'Tut, tut!' we say under our self-righteous breath as we read the salacious headlines. 'Who could imagine anybody doing such a thing?' The implication being, 'I never would.'

Our moral censure of others is once again just a device to distract attention from our own guilt. We think that by adopting a tone of shocked indignation over the sins of others, our own sin will go unnoticed. As Jesus put it, we point out the speck in other people's eyes in order to distract attention from the great plank in our own (Matthew 7:3). Or as the apostle Paul says, we try to escape judgment by making ourselves into judges (Romans 2:3). By this type of comparative obedience many of us will probably succeed today in avoiding the chastening effect of this very parable upon our lives.

Have you heard of the Sunday School teacher who told this story to his class? Afterwards he drew what he thought was the obvious moral lesson. 'Now, children,' he said, 'let's thank God we're not like that proud Pharisee.'

The trouble is it's all too easy for Christians to slip into the Pharisee's shoes without even realizing we are doing it, in the very act of *trying to* distance ourselves from him.

By these three classic techniques our Pharisee succeeds, then, in feeling good about himself. By these means he coped with his guilt feelings very well. So very well that they had been completely repressed. No flutter of moral anxiety disturbed this man's conscience at all. And yet Jesus insists that for all the effectiveness of his self-administered psychotherapy, his real guilt remained. It had not been diminished one jot. He *felt* all right, but his *feelings* did not correspond to the state of his soul. He might have been more emotionally stable as a result of his religious exercises, but he was nearer hell.

Am I not right, then, to be concerned that there may be many today suffering from the very same delusion? Or that I myself may be falling into this very same trap by using this parable to critique the religion of others when I should rather be examining myself? How do I deal with *my* guilt? That's the issue. Am I content simply to ease the pangs of conscience by persuading myself that 'I'm OK, thank you very much'? Or do I, like that tax man, yearn for some much more radical solution than that to the pollution of my soul?

This issue of handling guilt was brought home to me some years ago with peculiar force. I had to counsel a young university student who had just had an abortion to avoid the inconvenience of a pregnancy that would have interrupted her degree course. To her surprise she found herself overwhelmed with guilt in the aftermath of the operation. So devastated was she by what she had done that she had even attempted suicide, and that's why I'd been asked to see her. What do you say to a young woman like that?

I'll tell you what a lot of her friends were saying. 'Don't be so silly. You're just suffering from a form of post-natal depression. It's your hormones. You've got nothing to be ashamed of. Snap out of it! What's the difference between an abortion and a spontaneous miscarriage?'

Some of her colleagues were studying psychology, and had gladly analysed her guilt feelings in terms of Freud and Jung. She herself was a social scientist and was well aware of the argument that all moral convictions are just the result of human societal conditioning. Maybe if she'd looked hard enough she could have found some culture somewhere that regularly procured abortions without any conscience about it whatsoever. But she still felt guilty. And no amount of rationalizing would take the feeling away.

She had discovered what her friends, employing the modern secular equivalents of pharisaical religion, had succeeded in hiding from themselves: that guilt is real. It's not just a mental state. She did not want to be sent to the psychiatrist to get her guilt neurosis erased. She didn't want to be reassured with the smooth talk of some nondirective student counsellor. She didn't want to be deprogrammed like one of Pavlov's dogs. She wanted to be treated like a responsible human being. What she wanted was not some therapy to make her feel better, but an answer to the guilt she had incurred; a guilt which she was persuaded was not a psychological aberration, but an objective stain on her life. In a word, she wanted forgiveness.

She'd reached the same point of personal desperation as the tax man. He wouldn't rationalize his guilt away either. He wouldn't persuade himself that he wasn't so bad after all, or try to cloak his sin with legalistic observances or unfavourable comparisons with others. He made no feeble excuses, pleaded no mitigating circumstances, offered no compensatory penances. He simply begged: 'God, be merciful to me, a sinner.' And, says Jesus, that man went home not just feeling better, but with his moral status dramatically reversed in the eyes of God.

> *I tell you that this man, rather than the other, went home justified before God* (Luke 18:14).

'Justified' is a word not from the vocabulary of the psychiatrist but from the lawcourts. It does not describe how the tax man *felt*. It describes how he stood legally before God's bar of justice. It means quite literally that God had declared him innocent. Just as a judge might acquit an accused person, so God had passed a verdict of 'not guilty' on this conscience-stricken man. And Jesus would have us learn from this story that the discovery of such justification is what true religion is all about. It is the spiritual remedy by which we are liberated, not just from guilt feelings but from the fact of guilt. It's not merely a method for easing our consciences. Justification is about the cleansing of our lives. It's not a psychological analgesic. It is a moral purgative.

Martin Luther wrote, 'There are only two sorts of people in the world: sinners who think themselves righteous, and the righteous who think themselves sinners.' It's a bold generalization, as Luther's so often are, and it needs qualification if it's not to be misunderstood. But essentially he's right. And the Pharisee and tax man epitomize the point he's making.

Fundamentally the difference between these two was the grounds upon which they sought acquittal in the eyes of God. The Pharisee was one of those who, Luke observes, 'were confident of their own righteousness and looked down on everybody else' (18:9). He could make it to heaven by his own efforts. He would have nothing to be ashamed of before God's tribunal. Why, he'd be able to boast about how hard he had worked to get there!

How many tragic people there are in church every Sunday who tread that path! I sometimes think this is going to be the greatest irony of hell, that it will be full, not of shame or even regret, but of self-righteous indignation. Many of those there will be convinced that they don't deserve it. 'How dare God damn me,' they'll be saying, 'after all I did for him?' Sometimes I shudder to imagine the shock that there will be on that last day, as they present their self-manufactured ticket at the gate of heaven and hear it declared a counterfeit.

Why do they try it on? Jesus surely puts his finger on the nub of the matter in that postscript:

Everyone who exalts himself will be humbled, and he who humbles himself will be exalted (Luke 18:14).

It was conceit that lay at the root of the Pharisee's religion. He wanted to get to heaven with his dignity unscathed. He wanted to go through those pearly gates with his head held high. He wanted a righteousness he could be proud of. But no such righteousness exists. For, as a matter of unvarying policy on God's part, everyone who exalts himself will be humbled.

This is the essential lesson of Jesus's own example. He accepts the title 'Lord', but he takes the role of a servant. He shares equality with God, but he hangs voluntarily on a cross. No wonder he offended and perplexed people. In those days humility was a vice, a despicable sign of weakness. Yet Jesus insists that not only must *we* be humble; he reveals in his incarnation and in his passion that the heart of God himself is humble.

No wonder this Pharisee can't go to heaven, then; he is contemptuous of humility. By contrast, for the tax man it was his only hope of salvation: 'God, have mercy on me, a sinner' (Luke 18:13).

Again, 'mercy' is a weak translation, for it's not the normal word for 'mercy' at all. In fact if we were going to translate it accurately in English we'd have to use an old-fashioned phrase like 'be propitiated towards me'. This word was associated with the sacrificial ritual of the temple and had to do with atonement for sins.

This tax man's hope is not just in God's loving and compassionate character, you see. Remember where he is. His eyes are on the altar where the temple priest at the hour of prayer has just offered sacrifice for the sins of the people. 'Please, God,' he says, 'I see the bloodstains there on the altar. Accept that sacrifice on my behalf, be propitiated towards me.' He's not just appealing to God's better nature when he says, 'Be merciful to me.' He's laying claim to God's own remedy for the sinner's plight. And in doing so, he highlights one more vital lesson that a morally complacent world too easily forgets: that there can be no real assurance of pardon without an act of atonement that satisfies God.

Some people think that forgiveness is easy for God. 'Of

course God will forgive me,' they say, 'it's his business.' Not so. It's dreadfully hard for God to forgive sin. He's the moral governor of the universe. If he overlooks a sin it's as good as saying that sin doesn't matter. The integrity of his own righteousness means that he must disassociate himself from wickedness wherever he sees it. He can't lay himself open to the charge of moral indifference or moral inconsistency. If he did, he wouldn't be a righteous God any longer. And that's why in Old Testament times there had to be an altar, there had to be a sacrifice.

That sacrifice was first of all a symbol of the seriousness of sin in God's eyes. We human beings are squeamish about blood. Well, God is squeamish about sin. He is repulsed by its stench and stain. That blood sacrifice on the altar was the sign of his moral revulsion.

More than that, though: sacrifice was a symbol of the penalty for sin. For as blood speaks of death, so sin demands death. No less a price is adequate to express the horror and the indignation of a holy God. Forgiveness may be offered freely in the Bible, but never make the mistake of thinking it's cheap. The Bible knows nothing of cheap forgiveness. Our tax man realized that. 'Oh God,' he cried, 'be propitiated towards me, let my sin be atoned for. I don't minimize the seriousness of my crimes. I don't underestimate the penalty they deserve. I see the blood, I know the cost. So please, God, turn your anger from me; be satisfied that a sacrificial substitute has died on the altar in my place today. And so have mercy on me, the sinner.'

This may seem a strange question, but I fear I must ask it. Have you sought God's pardon the tax man's way, through God's merciful provision of an atoning sacrifice? Or do you seek a righteousness like the Pharisee's, built on your religious reputation and your moral achievements?

Extraordinary as it may sound, I find pastorally that there are an enormous number of professing Christians today who come to church regularly to pray and yet have never really made this most fundamental discovery. Deep down they know they are guilty, but instead of resolving their guilt God's way, they bury it.

The symptoms of that buried guilt are so easy to spot. A lack of self-esteem, a low self-image, an inferiority complex. They go around complaining, 'I'm no good at being a Christian. I don't feel excited about being a Christian, I've got no assurance of salvation, no joy in worship, no enthusiasm to witness. I'm a lame-duck Christian, that's what I am.' Countless people are burdened in this way. They say they're depressed, that they can't cope, that they always make a mess of things, that they're no use to anybody and it's pointless trying to improve themselves. What's wrong with these people? What's the source of this spiritual debility?

I don't want to oversimplify by generalization. The pastoral problems involved may be very complex. But I am convinced that a considerable proportion of these folk are suffering from unresolved feelings of repressed guilt. Christians though they are, or say they are, their attitudes are shaped by this guilt-denying world of ours. And as a result they have never been truly convicted of sin, never properly understood God's remedy for sin, and therefore have never really felt truly pardoned of sin. That's why they feel inadequate, that's why assurance eludes them. The one person you can never forgive is yourself. So long as this spectre of unacknowledged guilt deep within their psyche haunts them, they will continue to suffer the destructive consequences of subconscious self-hatred eating away inside them, destroying their motivation, their ambition, their assurance.

What's the answer? The answer is that they must come and stand where the tax man stood. Justification by faith must cease to be a cerebral article of their creed and become instead an experimental truth in their hearts. They must stand where the tax man stood, with all the defensive masks removed, all the illusions of moral respectability shattered, all pretence of self-righteousness abandoned. They must look where the tax man looked, to a sacrifice; but to a far nobler and more costly sacrifice than ever was slain on a temple altar. They must look to a cross where the Son of God himself shed his blood once and for all, to make atonement for the sin of the world. And they must pray as that tax man prayed, 'God, have mercy on me. I ask for no cheap forgiveness; I do not underestimate the seriousness of my crime. I know that the penalty of my sin is death, but please, God, be satisfied that a worthy substitute has paid the price in my place, and so be merciful to me, the sinner.'

And most of all, they need to hear that reassuring verdict of Jesus upon such a penitential prayer: 'I tell you that this man . . . went home justified' (Luke 18:14). He stood in the presence of God now not as a despised and condemned criminal, but as a beloved and accepted child. Justified by faith, he could now have peace with God. Not the peace of the Pharisee, that self-manufactured psychological fiction which would one day be stripped from him to his horror in final judgment. No, a peace with God based on God's own irreversible, incontestable declaration of pardon through Jesus' blood.

So much depends on how we deal with our guilt. Are we content merely with a little religious therapy that enables us to feel good about ourselves, or do we long for a radical cleansing of the real guilt that lies on our souls? It will depend on what sort of righteousness we seek. A righteousness of our own that comes through our own moral efforts, or a righteousness from God that depends on faith?

The theologian Karl Barth expresses the reason for our resistance to that divine remedy insightfully:

> We dislike hearing that we are saved by grace alone. We don't really appreciate that God does

not owe us anything, that we are bound to live from His goodness alone, that we are left with nothing but the great humility of a child presented with many gifts. To put it bluntly, we do not like to believe.

But believe we must. Believe in the greatness of the merciful heart of God. Believe in the sufficiency of Christ's atoning sacrifice. Believe most of all, perhaps, in the truth of that extraordinary promise, 'Everyone who exalts himself will be humbled, but he who humbles himself will be exalted.'

In the topsy-turvy world of heaven, it is the poor who are rich, the humbled who are great. In the paradoxical topography of the kingdom of God, the way up is down.

7

That Monday-morning feeling

Luke 19:11–27

_____

While they were listening to this, he went on to tell them a parable, because he was near Jerusalem and the people thought that the kingdom of God was going to appear at once. [12]He said: 'A man of noble birth went to a distant country to have himself appointed king and then to return. [13]So he called ten of his servants and gave them ten minas. "Put this money to work,"he said, "until I come back."

[14]*'But his subjects hated him and sent a delegation after him to say, "We don't want this man to be our king."*

[15]*'He was made king, however, and returned home. Then he sent for the servants to whom he had given the money, in order to find out what they had gained with it.*

[16]*'The first one came and said, "Sir, your mina has earned ten more."*

[17]*'"Well done, my good servant!" his master replied. "Because you have been trustworthy in a very small matter, take charge of ten cities."*

[18]*'The second came and said, "Sir, your mina has earned five more."*

[19]*'His master answered, "You take charge of five cities."*

[20]*'Then another servant came and said, "Sir, here is your mina; I have kept it laid away in a piece of cloth. [21]I was afraid of you, because you are a hard man. You take out what you did not put in and reap what you did not sow."*

[22]*'His master replied, "I will judge you by your own words, you wicked servant! You knew, did you, that I am a hard man, taking out what I did not put in, and reaping what I did not sow? [23]Why then didn't you put my money on deposit, so that when I came back, I could have collected it with interest?"*

[24]*'Then he said to those standing by, "Take his mina away*

from him and give it to the one who has ten minas."

25'"Sir," they said, "he already has ten!"

26'He replied, "I tell you that to everyone who has, more will be given, but as for the one who has nothing, even what he has will be taken away. 27But those enemies of mine who did not want me to be a king over them – bring them here and kill them in front of me."'

Most people find Mondays depressing. In fact, a team of European doctors and psychiatrists recently completed a study on the subject. They found that there is a higher chance of having a heart attack on Monday than on any other day of the week. That is not merely the result of over-indulgence during the weekend, for the incidence of every other kind of stress-related illness and condition is increased on Mondays too. Your blood pressure is elevated on Mondays, meaning that you have a higher risk of a stroke. Your stomach acidity will be higher, which means that you face a higher risk of having an ulcer. You will be glad to know, also, that you are twice as likely to commit suicide on a Monday as on any other day.

That Monday-morning feeling is no myth, but a medical fact. There can be only one explanation: a great many of us find the very idea of work depressing. It is easy to think that the reason for this is the pressure we are put under at work, the expectation to perform. For some high-flyers, I suppose, that is a contributory factor. It is not easy to keep your balance when you are surrounded by a workaholic culture. I remember a friend of mine telling me that he had only ever met three people who were absolutely obsessed with work. Unfortunately they happened to be the other three men in his office!

The Monday-morning syndrome, interestingly, is even more evident in the lives of low-flyers than it is in the lives of high-flyers. People with mundane, undemanding jobs display the same stress symptoms as people who have far more demanding occupations. Pressure therefore cannot be the whole story. Is the reason for that Monday-morning feeling, then, rather that our personal relationships at work generate anxiety? Maybe it's the cattiness among the girls in the typing-pool, or competitiveness among the men in the sales team. Could it be physical working conditions that are to blame? Would we be less vulnerable to stress if relaxing music was piped across the factory floor, or if the management invested in more comfortable office furniture?

There's no denying that social and environmental factors make a big difference to job satisfaction. Interestingly again, however, research shows that negative Monday-morning feelings are not necessarily reduced in companies which try very hard to create a pleasant working atmosphere. No, there's no escaping the conclusion of such findings, I'm afraid. No matter how good the job, how considerate your employer, how nice the people you work with, for a great many of us it is the very idea of work that is unpalatable. We do not want to do it. The thought of having to do it, which Monday morning forces upon us, is quite enough to plunge us into an emotional abyss.

Is our problem, then, mere laziness? Perhaps we are all congenitally idle. But surely the reason cannot be that simple either. Many studies have shown that redundancy and retirement are stress-inducing too, sometimes far more stress-inducing than the job we used to do. No doubt there are a few idle jacks in this world whose idea of bliss is a life of uninterrupted leisure, but actually the vast majority of us need work in order to feel fulfilled. In his book *Three Men in a Boat*, Jerome K. Jerome writes, 'I like work: it fascinates me. I can sit and look at it for hours.' He was being deliberately humorous, but there is a kind of deeper truth hidden in his wit. It is impossible, actually, to enjoy idleness unless you know there is work you could be doing. To be totally idle is not a recipe for bliss at all, but for despair. If you don't believe me, you ask the men and women in the Job Centre queue. That

Monday-morning feeling does not reflect laziness.

I suggest it is rather hopelessness, a hopelessness that has plenty to do but no satisfying reason for doing it. It is not possible to live a meaningful human life unless you believe something about the future. Alexander Pope was getting at it in his famous lines:

> Hope springs eternal in the human breast;
> Man never Is, but always To be blest.

To try to live without hope is like trying to play football without goalposts. You may dribble the ball with great skill, execute some fine passes, even enjoy the game to an extent. But what's the point of it all? Unless there's some purpose, some objective, some goal for human existence, the whole show is a monstrous farce. Stephen Crane's poem in *The Black Riders* expresses this point well:

> I saw a man pursuing the horizon;
> Round and round they sped.
> I was disturbed at this;
> I accosted the man.
> 'It is futile,' I said, 'You can never—'
> 'You lie,' he cried,
> And ran on.

That surely is the absurdity of much which we today so optimistically call 'progress'. You can talk about advancing only when you have a clear idea of where you are supposed to be going.

The dilemma of modern secular men and women is that we no longer possess such a sense of direction. It is like the counsel of despair adopted by the British government when it ruled Ireland during the potato blight. In order to sustain the morale of the people by providing employment, the British ordered the construction of unnecessary roads, roads that went nowhere.

Humanity at the end of the twentieth century is beginning to wonder if we haven't been unwittingly committing our energies to such a pointless enterprise for years. Woody Allen truthfully quipped, 'The future isn't what it used to be.' Optimism about the destiny of the human race has all but collapsed today. True, you still hear a few people mouthing the old utopian dreams about a future technological paradise on earth, but those who know most are not so stupid any longer. Such dreams lie buried under the carnage of two world wars and the Hiroshima cloud. Humanism has been discredited, and confidence in a future brought about by human science has died as a result.

Yet we human beings must have hope. We can't live without it. Children count the days till Christmas. Teenagers look forward to the next date with their boyfriend or girlfriend. Grown-ups revel in their holiday brochures. We have to have hope. Mere survival isn't enough for us. If we are going to endure the tedium and the fatigue of everyday life, we must have light on the horizon to steer by. A person without anything to look forward to is a person of utter despair.

Tony Hancock was a very fine comedian in the 1950s and 1960s. In his last TV monologue in 1964 he performed a piece which proved ironic.

> What have you achieved? What have you achieved? You lost your chance, me old son. You contributed absolutely nothing to this life. A waste of time you being here at all. No place for you in Westminster Abbey. The best you can expect is a few daffodils in a jam jar and a black stone bearing the legend, 'He came, and he went.' And in between? Nothing. Nobody will even notice you're not here. After about a year somebody might say down the pub, 'Where's old Hancock? I haven't seen him around lately.'

'Oh, he's dead, you know.'

'Is he?'

A right *raison d'être*, that is.

Poignantly, a couple of years after that final TV show, Tony Hancock himself committed suicide. The despair that he was articulating was evidently too close to the truth for comfort. Hope springs eternal? No, Mr Pope, I'm afraid it doesn't always. Sometimes hope dries up. When it does, it isn't just hope that's extinguished. A person, bereft of purpose, dies too. 'I have nothing to live for,' says the suicide note. Dante, in his *The Divine Comedy*, makes the inscription over the gate of hell read, 'All hope abandon, you who enter here!' There is nothing, absolutely nothing, quite so appalling and dreadful to the human spirit as to be irremediably hopeless.

What are you looking forward to? What is the point of your life? A lot of us manage to put on a façade of ambition and direction in life. We tell people we're happy and well adjusted, and that we know where we are going. But is it not the truth that the Monday-morning feeling gets us too? And if we really plumb those inner depths of personal honesty, the reason it gets us is that there is a vacuum inside us. We do *not* know where we are going. We do not have anything important or big enough to live for, nothing bigger than the next party, the next disco, or the next date.

In the 1960s and 1970s, quite a lot of young people dropped out of careers and study, part in protest, and part in despair at this sense of hopelessness. The rat-race, they said, was an exercise in futility. The 1980s witnessed a revived commitment to competing in the rat-race. But the fundamental question those earlier drop-outs asked was never really answered. What is the point of slogging your guts out for forty-two and a half hours a week, forty-nine weeks a year? Whether the job is demanding or boring, whether the atmosphere is friendly or hostile, whether the salary is high or low, surely the truth is, as Tony Hancock so sadly said, that it is all a monumental waste of time. Shakespeare expressed it eloquently when he said:

> Life's but a walking shadow, a poor player,
> That struts and frets his hour upon the stage,
> And then is heard no more; it is a tale
> Told by an idiot, full of sound and fury,
> Signifying nothing.

The operative word is that final 'nothing'. The Monday-morning feeling is the stress, anxiety, and depression we feel when we are confronted with that nothingness. It is not the prospect of hard labour that moves us to bury our heads under the bedclothes, and to roll ourselves up into a secure foetal position, praying for the night to return. Rather, it is the prospect of futility. And if that analysis is correct, there is only one way to escape those Monday-morning blues. That is to discover some meaning to life. If we can find some context of hope, then not only our daily work, but every aspect of our human existence, can find meaning and direction.

It is this quest which makes the parable of the ten minas so interesting and important. In it Jesus provides us with that vital future perspective which we need to give our work significance. His tale tells us that history is going somewhere; you and I are going somewhere. Life is not just a labyrinth without an exit. There is a goal to existence. And because there is, Monday morning need never depress us again. There is something worth living for, and therefore something worth working for.

Luke sets the scene for us in the earlier part of chapter 19. Jesus tells the parable 'because he was near Jerusalem and the people thought that the kingdom of God was going to appear at once' (verse 11).

Jesus had been travelling slowly and deliberately towards the capital city of Jerusalem for some months.

Luke structures the whole of his gospel from 9:51 onwards around that journey. Among Jesus' companions there have been signs of escalating anticipation. They all sense that Jesus' life is moving towards a crisis. Everyone feels that when they get to Jerusalem something absolutely dramatic is going to happen. Here in Luke 19, they have reached Jericho, less than 20 miles from the capital, and it is clear that by now the atmosphere of expectancy has intensified to fever pitch. The people thought the kingdom of God was going to appear at any moment.

The prophets in the Old Testament had told the Jewish people about this 'kingdom' to come. It would mean that the world would be ruled not simply by God's sovereign providence the way it is now. In the kingdom of God, the world would be ruled by God's direct, theocratic command through his chosen Messiah. Some of Jesus' followers, however, were convinced that he was the Messiah. 'You've seen what miraculous signs he's been doing,' they whispered to one another. 'It can only be a few days now before he sets up the kingdom of God we've all been waiting for. I can't wait to see the look on the faces of those Roman tyrants, can you? It's nearly here!'

To give him his due, Jesus had tried on a number of occasions to put an end to such hysteria. Repeatedly he had warned his disciples that it was death that awaited him in Jerusalem, not political triumph. In fact, he had said as much just before they arrived in Jericho. But the disciples, it seems, couldn't take it in. They didn't want to accept such uncongenial words. So they did nothing to quench the rising tide of popular euphoria.

Jesus, sensing that things were getting a bit out of control, decided that he must take some action. As so often in previous situations, what he did was to tell a story, one of his matchless 'Stealth bomber' parables. In the past, he has launched these secret weapons of his in order to explode the complacency and the self-righteousness of the religious Establishment. This time, however, the target audience is different. This tale belongs to a family of parables which Jesus told, not with the purpose of challenging the Pharisees and the scribes, but rather with the purpose of instructing his own followers about the nature of the kingdom of God. As we said in chapter 1, the Jews of Jesus' day expected the kingdom of God to come in a single shattering moment, like a thunderbolt from heaven. Jesus, in his parables of the kingdom, makes it clear that God's strategy is actually going to be rather different from that popular expectation. The kingdom of God was going to come in a way unforeseen by the Jewish people: in three phases rather than in a single apocalyptic crisis.

It is this phased strategy that Jesus is trying once again to get across in the opening of this parable.

> *A man of noble birth went to a distant country to have himself appointed king and then to return* (Luke 19:12).

The point of the metaphor is that Jesus, heir of the world though he is, will not claim the kingdom immediately. He has a long journey to travel before he can enjoy his coronation. He must leave this world altogether. Only on his return will he be publicly enthroned. In the meantime, during the period of his absence, he is leaving those who count themselves as his servants a task.

> *He called ten of his servants and gave them ten minas. 'Put this money to work,' he said, 'until I come back'* (Luke 19:13).

If the disciples were expecting victory the moment they set foot in Jerusalem, they would be disappointed, then. Soon after they arrived there, Jesus would be leaving them. But they were not to be disheartened about that. He had a farewell endowment for them, modest by comparison with the vast wealth that he would have at his disposal when he returned in glory, but substantial enough to test the faithfulness of his servants and their sense of responsibility. In the short term, that is what the future holds for them. He is not offering them immediate access to messianic power and glory. What he is offering them is an opportunity for service.

Here then is Jesus' answer to the dreaded Monday-morning feeling. 'Put this money to work until I come back.' This, if you like, is the Bible's work ethic. Notice, it is grounded not in mere moral duty, but in future hope. We are to put his money to work *until he comes back.* The final phrase is desperately important.

The world is going somewhere, the king is returning. Make the most, then, of the opportunities and the resources you have to invest in his kingdom by working hard for him. That is Jesus' message.

People divide themselves into three broad categories, depending on how they respond to that challenge. At one extreme are those who identify themselves as rebels; his subjects hated him and sent a delegation after him to say, 'We don't want this man to be our king' (Luke 19:14). Jesus' fellow countrymen would relate very easily to this scenario, because just a few years before, after the death of Herod the Great, his son Archelaus went to Rome to ask Augustus Caesar to make him king over Judea. But Herod the Great's dynasty was very unpopular among many of the Jews. The Jews therefore sent a delegation of fifty senior men to oppose the appointment. It may very well be that this rebellion in the story resonated with the Herod affair in the memories of many Jews at that time. Jesus is saying that people would reject God's Messiah too, resenting his interference in their affairs.

Some of them might cloak their rebellion in the guise of doubt or ignorance. But Jesus is adamant that the root of this resistance to his rule is not intellectual but moral. It lies not in the mind, but in the will. 'We don't want this man to be our king.' That's what they would say. Such rebels wave their impudent fists in vain. For as the story recounts, 'He was made king, however, and returned home.' Jesus' point is that nothing can stop his final triumph. Indeed, at the very end of the parable, he tells us what fate befell these rebels as a result of their unwillingness to accept the king: 'Those enemies of mine who did not want me to be a king over them – bring them here and kill them in front of me' (Luke 19:27).

Like me, I expect you find that a very harsh ending, an ending in some ways we would rather Jesus had left out. The fact is, however, that there can be no room in the kingdom of heaven for rebels. It was rebellion against God that ruined this world in the first place. We human beings arrogantly thought that we could defy God's commandment with impunity. And look what a mess we have made of the world as a result!

God is determined that his new world is not going to suffer the same fate. It is going to be populated only by those who acknowledge, desire and appreciate his sovereign rule. The very foundation of that new age to come will be the prayer, 'Your kingdom come, your will be done' (Matthew 6:10). Those who are not willing to pray such a prayer exclude themselves from it. They make it clear that they would not be happy in his kingdom. Why, if God let them in they would ruin it within twenty-four hours! Sure, it is a harsh verdict: 'Bring them here and kill them in front of me.' But by it Jesus conveys the hard truth that if we do not want this king, then we cannot have a role in his kingdom.

A second category of people, at the other extreme, are those whom Jesus called in his parable 'the good servants'.

He sent for the servants to whom he had given the money, in order to find out what they had gained with it.

> The first one came and said, 'Sir, your mina has earned ten more.'
>
> 'Well done, my good servant!' his master replied. 'Because you have been trustworthy in a very small matter, take charge of ten cities.'
>
> The second came and said, 'Sir, your mina has earned five more.'
>
> His master answered, 'You take charge of five cities' (Luke 19:15–19).

Again, this is an important element of the story. For there are two mistakes people habitually make about going to heaven. The first mistake is to think that you can get to heaven by good works. The second is to think you can get to heaven *without* good works. There are few tensions in the Bible more important to grasp than that which holds this apparent contradiction together.

On the one hand, the Bible insists that we cannot earn our salvation. This was demonstrated in Jesus' parable of the Pharisee and the tax man in the temple. The only way any of us can be acquitted is on the basis of God's grace. Forgiveness is a gift he bestows out of all proportion to any merit we could possibly claim. On the other hand, the Bible insists also that our actions are relevant to our eternal destiny. Though we can't *earn* God's grace, we can and we ought to give *evidence* of it in our lives.

Part of the purpose of this parable in Luke 19 is to draw to our attention the importance of that practical evidence. Clearly, Jesus thinks it will not be enough on the last day simply to put our hands up and say, 'I'm here, Lord!' Rather, when the Book of Life is opened there must be something to show, some evidence of our commitment, of our faith, of our response, as in the case of this first man who comes in. 'Sir, your mina has earned ten more.'

Notice the king's response. 'Well done . . . good servant . . . you have been trustworthy.' There is ambiguity in that word translated 'trustworthy'. It can mean either 'reliable' or 'believing'. Those two meanings are of course not disconnected, for we show that we are believers by the obedience of our lives. The two qualities hang together. In vain do we pretend that we 'trust', if we are not trustworthy servants.

Jesus, of course, is using a financial metaphor to describe the trustworthiness for which God is looking. What precisely does he mean by this 'mina' which the Master has given to his servants? Some suggest it is a symbol for the Holy Spirit, others that it symbolizes the gospel message. Still others suggest that it stands for any sort of talent, gift, or endowment that an individual might possess and hold in trust for God.

The answer is, I suppose, that it can be all of those things. The mina is what Jesus has left us with in his absence – the resources, the endowments, the charge, the mandate, which he has given us to be getting on with now that he has returned to heaven.

By the same token, the cities which are placed under the servants' jurisdiction as a reward for their faithfulness are also clearly symbolic. Jesus is not suggesting here that heaven will be territorially parcelled out as if he were Henry VIII awarding political patronage to his favourites. The cities in the story stand for the fact that the use we make of our resources and opportunities, here, in this period of time, while we're waiting for his return, can have and will have eternal consequences. It is possible, he's saying, to live here and now in such a way that heaven will be enriched for us.

How can that be? What is the nature of this reward which he pictures in the gift of cities? The Bible does not spell that out very clearly. Jesus elsewhere talks about 'laying up treasure in heaven', but never completely explains just what that celestial treasure is. What he is clear about is that it is possible to live our lives now directed in such a way that what we achieve lasts. It is not all thrown away. The mark of good servants is that they do make a wise, long-term investment.

That is good news in a world that is full of Monday-morning depression. It is good news that we can work our guts out in the service of Jesus Christ, and know that this counts. As Jesus said on one occasion, 'If anyone gives even a cup of cold water to one of these little ones . . . he will certainly not lose his reward' (Matthew 10:42). Paul develops this thought in his letter to the Colossians. He says it doesn't matter what your job is, or what role you fulfil in society. You might be a slave or a master, you might be a husband or a wife, you might be a parent or a child. Every Christian can dedicate his or her role or job to Christ, and should do so. Whatever you do, he urges, do it from the heart as working for the Lord. It makes sense, he insists, because it is from the Lord that ultimately we expect our reward (Colossians 3:18 – 4:1).

The Christian is going somewhere, with a goal, with a hope. That means that our work has significance even though it may be mundane – even though, as in the case of a slave in the Roman Empire, it could be positively degrading.

There is a story of three workmen on a building site. A TV interviewer asks them what they are doing. The first man replies, rather unimaginatively, 'Oh, I'm breaking rock.' The second replies, somewhat more thoughtfully, 'I'm earning money to feed my wife and kids.' Then he asks the third man. 'Oh,' he says, 'I'm building a cathedral.' It makes all the difference, you see, to have a goal, to see your life in an eternal perspective, to have hope.

There is a third category of response to the challenge of the coming kingdom, however: that of the wicked servant.

> Then another servant came and said, 'Sir, here is your mina; I have kept it laid away in a piece of cloth. I was afraid of you, because you are a hard man. You take out what you did not put in and reap what you did not sow.'

His master replied, 'I will judge you by your own words, you wicked servant!' (Luke 19:20–22).

The first thing to say about this servant is that his characterization of the master is grossly unfair. He is trying to make out that the master is some kind of vicious exploiter of the working classes, always looking to make a fast buck. But it's quite clear that he's nothing of the kind. He has entrusted ten servants with the equivalent of £50,000 or more. Remember, these were slaves – they didn't even have the status of an employee in the ancient world. Yet he commits to them this considerable wealth, putting it at their disposal to use while he's away. What's more, the reward which he grants to the first two servants on his return makes it quite clear that, far from being exploitative and ruthless, this man is a benefactor. He is only too willing to share with these slaves not just the management of his estate while it is convenient to him, but the enjoyment of his estate now that he has come into his full inheritance.

The third servant, in his acrimonious slander of the master's character, is simply projecting on to him his own mean-minded and mercenary disposition, it seems to me. He is embittered by something, perhaps his status as a slave. Maybe he feels some deep resentment at being given only £5,000 to play with, believing he could have done with more. Perhaps he is conscious that the other slaves have made rather better use of their money than he has, and feels somewhat peeved. Whatever the reason, the result is that he can't bring himself to believe in the kindness and generosity of the master. His behaviour is sulky. He wraps the money up in a handkerchief; 'I was afraid' is the excuse he offers. In a sense he was, I suppose, afraid that he might not be successful, afraid he would fail.

A traveller in the southern states of the USA once stopped in a small township. He paused to talk to one of the farmers sitting at the entrance of his home. 'How's your cotton coming along?' said the traveller.

'Ain't got none,' was the reply.

'Didn't you plant any?'

'No,' he said. 'Afraid of the boll-weevil.'

'How's your corn, then?'

'Didn't plant none. 'Fraid there weren't going to be no rain.'

'How about your potatoes?'

'Ain't got none. 'Fraid of the potato blight.'

'Well, what did you plant, then?'

'Nothin'. This year I figured I'd just play safe.'

This was the third servant's policy. He figured that he would just play safe. The irony was that he was playing very dangerously indeed. In trying to avoid the wrath of his master, which he said he feared so much, he was actually incurring that wrath to a far greater degree.

> *'I will judge you by your own words, you wicked servant! You knew, did you, that I am a hard man, taking out what I did not put in, and reaping what I did not sow? Why then didn't you put my money on deposit, so that when I came back, I could have collected it with interest?'* (Luke 19:22–23).

The master responds that even if he was the cruel tyrant the servant wanted to make him out to be, he had not acted accordingly. The servant had not even lived by that partial and distorted knowledge of his master that he had. His problem was not that he feared the master too much, but that he did not fear him half enough. If he had, he would have done something with that mina he had given him, even if it was only putting it in the bank. The truth was that he was a wicked servant, looking for an excuse for his sloth, negligence and irresponsibility.

What did Jesus mean when he said that the servant could have gone to the bankers with the money? Some, no doubt, will see this statement as New Testament approval for the stock market and for finance houses.

That, however, would be a most precarious conclusion to draw. If anything, in fact, this part of the story implies that taking money at interest is the action typical of an opportunist entrepreneur – the hard man who likes to gather what he has not sown, or, as we would say, get something for nothing. He is the sort of person who is interested in putting money out for interest. In Jesus' day, usury (that is, taking interest on loans) was regarded as immoral among the Jewish community. There's little doubt, therefore, that Jesus' hearers would have perceived this reference to money-lenders as pejorative.

Some have suggested therefore that in the story's original setting, the 'bankers' represent the Pharisees. It stands for those who wanted to keep the truth of God within the bounds of Israel and not share it with the world. Because a Jew couldn't lend money at interest, the only way you could have dealings with a banker was if you mixed with Gentiles. So, they suggest, what Jesus means when he says 'Go to the bankers' is 'Go to the Gentiles'. He is alluding to the responsibility the Jews bore to represent the truth of God to the pagan world, and this wicked and lazy servant hadn't done it.

There may be an element of truth in this theory, but I suspect that, certainly for us who are not first-century Jews, Jesus' teaching has a wider application than that. What he is saying, surely, is simply that there is a need for enterprise and energy in our use of the resources God has entrusted to us. By the example of his wicked servant, Jesus is warning us against insularity, parochialism, laziness, and passivity. He's telling us that we must work for his kingdom with vision and vigour. He's encouraging us to have enough confidence in God to believe that he will not treat us badly if 'in good faith' we make a mistake in our investment. God will recognize that there are risks in any enterprise. Only by taking such risks can you prosper in God's service. We mustn't allow fear to make us withdraw tortoise-like into the security of our shell. We must be prepared to commit ourselves in bold initiatives for the kingdom of God. If you like, Jesus is warning us here against an excessive conservatism. We are not, of course, rashly to throw our master's money around. That is not what he wanted from this servant. But Jesus is saying that we have a responsibility to make courageous decisions for the furthering of Christ's rule.

Some of us who are conservative theologically also tend to be conservative in every other way. We are happy to attend church every week, and to feel secure and cosy in the company of our Christian friends. Any exposure to the world, that nasty, wicked world, makes us feel decidedly uneasy. So we stay on the side-lines as spectators of the enterprise of others.

But in this tale, Jesus is surely warning us that it is only participants who win the prize. *The Sacred Diary of Adrian Plass* has a relevant section in this connection:

> Sunday January 12th. Six-fruit-gum talk on witnessing by Edwin this morning. Very good. Made you want to go straight out and witness to somebody. Drifted off into a pleasant day-dream in which I began to preach in the street and ended up with a huge crowd of people all repenting in tears and being healed of their sickness just by the touch of my hand. Very near to tears myself during the chorus that followed, as I pictured myself addressing vast assemblies of needy people throughout the world. Came to with a shock as I realised that Edwin was asking for people to volunteer to do some actual street evangelism next Friday. Sat as low down in my seat as I could, trying to look like someone whose earnest desire to evangelize was thwarted by a previous appointment.

We all know that feeling. Perhaps the servant felt

irritated because he hadn't been given enough resources. If only he'd been given £50,000 instead of just £5,000, he could have made a real killing on the market. But what could he do with such a measly sum? It wasn't worth even trying.

Some of us, perhaps, would say something similar of our opportunity for Christian service. 'If I could preach like Billy Graham I'd be an evangelist. If I was any good at languages I'd be a missionary. If I was musical I'd join the choir or play in a band. If I was academic I'd go to theological college. If I wasn't so shy I'd start a Bible study group in my house. But God has given me so little, it's not worth trying.'

There is a story of the two little Cockney boys who were protesting their life-long devotion to each other. The first little boy said to the other, 'Hey, Bobby, if you 'ad a million pounds, would you give me 'alf?'

' 'Course I would,' he said.

'What about if you 'ad a fousand pounds?'

'I'd give you 'alf just the same.'

'What about if you 'ad a fousand marbles?'

'I'd give you 'alf of 'em,' he replied.

'What about if you 'ad *two* marbles?'

(*Pause*.) 'That's jolly well not fair. You know I've *got* two marbles.'

God wants our two marbles. He is not interested in the hypothetical devotion which we would exercise if only we had got masses of resources, endowments and spiritual gifts at our disposal. He wants our two marbles dedicated in his service. Only thus will we have something to show, he says, on the last day, as evidence that we are men and women of faith, and trustworthy, good servants.

> *Then he said to those standing by, 'Take his mina away from him and give it to the one who has ten minas.'*
> *'Sir,' they said, 'he already has ten!'*

*He replied, 'I tell you that to everyone who has,
more will be given, but as for the one who has
nothing, even what he has will be taken away'* (Luke
19:24–26).

This is surely unfair. Why should his mina be given to
the one who has already got plenty? The servant must
have meant well.

Jesus, however, illustrates a spiritual principle here
which he repeats many times: that you cannot find eternal
life by trying to hang on to what you've got. The only
people who are going to discover real life as God intends
us to live it are those who are willing to throw their lives
away. People who hang on to their lives, greedily
hoarding what God has given them, are going to finish
up losing it altogether. The people who are going to
receive, paradoxically, are the people who are willing to
let go, to put at risk themselves and what God has given
them. There is no special half-way house on the day of
judgment for those who meant well.

Luke's account of the story actually leaves the final
destiny of this man in some doubt. He does seem to draw
a line between the fate of the wicked servant who forfeits
his reward and the fate of the rebels who forfeit their
lives, but it may not be wise to pin too much hope on that
distinction. For in Matthew's version of this same story,
there is a far less optimistic end. 'Throw that worthless
servant outside, into the darkness, where there will be
weeping and gnashing of teeth' (Matthew 25:30).

The irony of this faithless servant is that in trying to
avoid taking risks, he was in fact taking the biggest
gamble of all – gambling with his soul.

It will soon be Monday again! We could wake up
depressed and miserable as people who are going
nowhere, or motivated and ambitious as people who
know we're going somewhere. The choice is ours.

8

The ultimate insult

Luke 20:9–19

He went on to tell the people this parable: 'A man planted a vineyard, rented it to some farmers and went away for a long time. [10]At harvest time he sent a servant to the tenants so they would give him some of the fruit of the vineyard. But the tenants beat him and sent him away empty-handed. [11]He sent another servant, but that one also they beat and treated shamefully and sent away empty-handed. [12]He sent still a third, and they wounded him and threw him out.

[13]"Then the owner of the vineyard said, "What shall I do? I will send my son, whom I love; perhaps they will respect him."

[14]'But when the tenants saw him, they talked the matter over. "This is the heir," they said. "Let's kill him, and the inheritance will be ours." [15]So they threw him out of the vineyard and killed him.

'What then will the owner of the vineyard do to them? [16]He will come and kill those tenants and give the vineyard to others.'

When the people heard this, they said, "May this never be!"

[17]Jesus looked directly at them and asked, 'Then what is the meaning of that which is written:

*'"The stone the builders rejected
    has become the capstone"?*

[18]Everyone who falls on that stone will be broken to pieces, but he on whom it falls will be crushed.'

[19]The teachers of the law and the chief priests looked for a way to arrest him immediately, because they knew he had spoken this parable against them. But they were afraid of the people.

G. K. Chesterton once commented that it's always easier to forgive an accidental injury than a deliberate insult. Some people do just seem to have the knack of opening their mouth and putting their foot in it. Everywhere they go they quite unintentionally make offensive and tactless remarks. But usually it's not too difficult to laugh off such clumsy insensitivity, precisely because we know they don't really mean it.

On the other hand, some insults are deliberate, premeditated and calculated to hurt, and they can deliver devastating emotional wounds especially if those who deliver them are people close to us. I remember some years ago being shown a letter written by a daughter to her mother. It was the most concentrated verbal vitriol I have ever read, and it broke that poor mother's heart. If her daughter had publicly spat in her face she could not have felt more profoundly humiliated.

'Sticks and stones may break my bones, but words can never hurt me.' That was the standard playground retort for such oral malice when I was at school. But the bluff is as poor as the rhyme, for names do hurt. Words have a capacity to draw tears and prey upon our minds, to sting our feelings in a way that no physical blow ever could.

Chesterton then is surely right. Perhaps a memory of some such slap in the face haunts you. If so, you'll be able to empathize profoundly with this final parable. In Luke 20 Jesus is telling us the story of what I reckon can justly be called the most shameless, the most cruel insult ever administered in the history of the world. I've called it 'the ultimate insult'. No other insult has demonstrated more brazen impertinence, left such permanent scars or been so totally undeserved. For this insult was delivered not against a human being but against the loving heart of God himself.

And Jesus tells us about it in the last of his parables which Luke records and which I think may well have been the last parable that Jesus ever told.

Some have argued that 'parable' is a misnomer for this story, for it comes closer to being a true allegory than any of the other stories that we've studied. It's also considerably less cryptic. You don't have to struggle to interpret this one. Perhaps it is because Jesus is now only a matter of days from the end of his life that he feels that he can speak with more transparency than he's done before. So obvious is the meaning of this story that even unsympathetic listeners are in no doubt about what Jesus is getting at. I want us to examine it in three stages.

1. How Jesus understood the human condition

A man planted a vineyard . . . (Luke 20:9).

Jesus told this parable in the context of another inquisition being conducted against him by the chief priests and the teachers of the law. His journey to Jerusalem, which Luke has been narrating since chapter 9, is at last complete. He has now entered the city amid a triumphant procession of his followers. And no sooner has he arrived than he causes a minor sensation by throwing the merchants out of the temple. Not surprisingly, the Jewish Establishment feel that some kind of official enquiry into this hothead's dubious credentials is required. Hence their loaded question, recorded by Luke earlier in the chapter:

'Tell us by what authority you are doing these things . . . Who gave you this authority?' (Luke 20:2).

Jesus, however, demonstrates once again his consummate skill in parrying this kind of hostile interrogation. He asks a loaded question of his own, refusing to answer theirs directly.

'Tell me, John's baptism – was it from heaven, or from men?' (20:4).

While they are fumbling to find a diplomatic answer which will not in some way incriminate or embarrass them, he goes straight on to tell his story.

It's a story which, we are told, his inquisitors were convinced was directed against them personally. I'm sure they weren't victim to any irrational paranoia in entertaining that suspicion. Anyone familiar with the Old Testament knew that the imagery of the vineyard which Jesus uses was not original. He had borrowed it. The prophet Isaiah, 800 years earlier, composed an allegorical song along very similar lines to Jesus' parable here. And the relationship between the two is unmistakable.

> My loved one had a vineyard
>   on a fertile hillside.
> He dug it up and cleared it of stones
>   and planted it with the choicest vines.
> He built a watchtower in it
>   and cut out a winepress as well.
> Then he looked for a crop of good grapes,
>   but it yielded only bad fruit.
>   (Isaiah 5:1–5)

Isaiah, however, interprets his allegory:

> The vineyard of the LORD Almighty
>   is the house of Israel,
> and the men of Judah
>   are the garden of his delight.
>   (Isaiah 5:7)

Isaiah's song was far too famous, and the parallels with Jesus' parable far too obvious, for the implication to be lost on these Jewish Bible scholars. The vineyard of which Jesus' parable speaks was the same as Isaiah's. It was Israel, the people of God. The one who planted this vineyard had to be God himself. The servants he had sent as emissaries were clearly the prophets of the Old Testament. And the wicked tenants to whom Jesus attributes the blame for the vineyard's unproductiveness: who are they? Well, one did not need to use much imagination to realize that they represent Israel's leaders, the very chief priests and teachers of the law who were trying to discredit Jesus at that moment. They were fully justified in thinking it was preached against them.

It wasn't the first time that Jesus had publicly denounced the hierarchy of his nation in this way. Back in Luke 11 there is a pungent attack, including one comment that you could almost regard as a commentary on this parable:

> *Woe to you [experts in the law], because you build tombs for the prophets, and it was your forefathers who killed them. So you testify that you approve of what your forefathers did; they killed the prophets and you build their tombs. Because of this, God in his wisdom said, 'I will send them prophets and apostles, some of whom they will kill and others they will persecute'* (Luke 11:47–49).

It is that strange divine strategy of sending his servants to a rejecting people that Jesus is allegorizing here in his story. The people of God refused to yield the fruit of righteousness which he requires of them. Instead they cruelly reject his servants the prophets whenever he sends them.

The danger for us, of course, is that in recognizing that the immediate reference of this parable was to Israel and to its leaders, we may evade its applications for us. We may say to ourselves perhaps, just as we did with the parable of the Pharisee and the tax man: 'Ah, those hypocritical high priests and scribes! We all know what wicked people they were. Thank God we are not among the wicked tenants he speaks about.' And once again, the shock and the rebuke of the parable is lost on us. We do not feel its stinging force.

That would be a disastrous mistake. For this parable of Jesus is no more limited in its relevance to the Israel of the first century AD than the song of Isaiah, which Jesus is expounding, was limited to the Israel of the eighth century BC. No, this is a story of privilege abused, generosity despised and responsibility shirked. And as such, I suggest, it speaks to the human condition generally. Luke certainly doesn't include it in his gospel to foster anti-Semitic prejudice among his Gentile readers. He included it because it was relevant to them.

I suggest to you that Jesus is not just describing Israel when he speaks of this vineyard. He is describing for us any and every situation on this fallen and rebellious planet where divine blessing is answered by human contempt. As such his words are of relevance to the visible church, a church which possesses the revelation of the Word of God in a way far beyond anything Israel ever knew, but which again and again grieves the heart of God with its apostasy.

These words are relevant to this land of Britain, a land which has experienced the influence of God in a way far beyond the majority of the nations, but which today is almost as secularized and pagan as some which have never heard the gospel.

It's relevant to some of us too as individuals. For we have been blessed personally through the ministry of the Word of God, far beyond many of our neighbours. Yet like that seed which was sown in thorny ground, it has produced so little fruit of obedience in our lives. Indeed, I don't think it's an overstatement to say that Jesus is describing for us here in this parable the tragic condition of the whole world. This is a world which was originally created by God, full of productive potential; it is like a farm prepared with everything needed for prosperity, planted and equipped, needing only to be worked. God put Adam in the garden to till it and keep it for him, we are told in Genesis 2.

So what's gone wrong with our world? Why have things turned sour and all our hopes foundered? Why do those optimistic dreams of a better society prove again and again to be elusive fantasies, like mirages in the desert?

A hundred years ago, at the very end of the nineteenth century, humanist intellectuals spoke with Promethean confidence about the glorious future that awaited the human race in the twentieth century: freedom from illness, war, poverty. The human race, guided by science and technology, they said, was on a route to a new golden age. They were sure of it. Everybody believed it. But instead, of course, these last hundred years have seen military conflict on an unprecedented global scale. They have witnessed famines of unparalleled dimensions. And as for freedom from illness, the medical science which has conquered smallpox and tuberculosis finds itself in the 1990s helpless before the pandemic scourge of the Aids virus.

Now in the 1990s, just as in the 1890s, there are those who, encouraged by the arrival not just of a new century but of a new millennium, speak once more in utopian terms about the dawn of a 'New Age'. Strange, isn't it, how that row of noughts on the end of the year 2000 is invested with almost mystical significance?

I wonder under what twenty-first century horrors that optimism is going to be buried in our children's lifetimes. It doesn't bear thinking about. The idyllic dream of the Garden of Eden keeps returning to haunt the human race, but it is nothing but a dream, a tantalizing, unrealizable dream of paradise lost. Why is it, Jesus, that we human beings are forever more insecure and violent, the further we advance? What's gone wrong in the vineyard, Jesus?

Is it that these tenant farmers have not yet evolved sufficiently from their animal origins to cooperate harmoniously in tending the vines? Is that the problem? Is it that their science is too primitive; do they need to update their productive efficiency with mechanization and fertilizers? Is it the vicious socio-economic system to which they are victim, with its oppressive absentee landlords and exploited labourers, seething with class antagonism?

No. According to Jesus it's none of these things. The problem is simple, he says. These people were placed in the vineyard as tenants, but they want to be owners.

> 'This is the heir,' they said. 'Let's kill him, and the inheritance will be ours' (Luke 20:14).

A tenant, of course, is accountable to somebody. He pays the rent. And Jesus is saying here that the same is true of human beings. We are accountable too. We owe a debt of moral obedience to the God who gave us this beautiful world to live in. That's why the word 'ought' features so prominently in our vocabulary. Originally the word 'ought' was part of the verb 'to owe'. It is the word of moral duty, of moral debt. Intuitively, all human beings recognize its authority over them. We can distinguish quite easily in our decision-making between what we want to do, what's easiest to do or what others are forcing us to do and what we ought to do.

And we instinctively feel that final constraint upon our choices has an unquestionable priority over all others. No matter how painful or inconvenient it may be, no matter how many people are trying to make me do the opposite, if something is what I *ought* to do then I *ought* to do it. I'm obliged by an imperative taking precedence over every other consideration. We all understand that word 'ought', for it is the word of our tenancy, the word of our obligation.

The question that has occupied the minds of philosophers for thousands of years, of course, is: where does this extraordinary sense of obligation come from? Increasingly, people want to relate it to social conditioning. 'Morality?' they say. 'Oh, that's just a social convention. We're taught certain things in our infancy, and we internalize them in the form of a conscience as we grow up.' But the trouble is that once you really believe that that's all morality is, it immediately loses its cogency and has no power over you. If right and wrong are just human inventions, then why shouldn't we disregard them if we want to?

Modern sociological analysis of the word 'ought' doesn't so much explain our sense of moral obligation as explain it away. Increasingly in our western world we are experiencing the anarchy and the permissiveness that irresistibly result from that sort of corrosive scepticism. For the distinctive thing about the word 'ought' is that it has to come from outside us, from some higher authority. And the problem with the humanistic philosophy that has dominated our culture for the last two centuries is that it has no access to such a higher authority. Its followers want a moral law but without a moral law-giver. They want personal values without a personal God. And you can't have them.

Responsibility by definition involves two parties. You have to be able to answer the question, 'Responsibility to whom?' Humanism can't answer that. That's why it's been such a disastrous interlude in our intellectual history.

But Jesus can answer the question. He understands where the word 'ought' comes from. It's from the owner of the vineyard, he says. Our moral nature just reflects the fact that we were put on this earth as tenants, not as owners. We owe something to our Creator. There is an inescapable 'ought' in the very nature of our human existence. The fundamental reason the vineyard is in a mess, he says, is that men and women, Jews, Gentiles or whoever they may be, habitually run away from that accountability. 'You can be a god too,' the devil told Eve.

And in our arrogance we believe the lie and choose the path of moral defiance rather than moral obedience (see Genesis 3:1–6).

In this respect the Jews' rejection of the prophets is not essentially different from our human rejection of God generally. Paul argues that very point in his letter to the Romans. Deep down, he says, we all know enough of our responsibility to God to submit our lives to his rule. The Jew has the Bible, the Gentile has his conscience. We are all without excuse. We are all sinners. We are all tenants in arrears with the rent (see Romans 1 – 3). And that's why the owner intervenes in our lives. And when he does, that's why our immediate reaction, like the tenants in the parable, is not one of surprise but of resistance.

Jesus would surely have us realize that in our twentieth century, exactly the same kind of illegitimate bid for moral autonomy that led to the failure of Israel is leading to the failure of our secular vision for a better world.

Here's the root of those ecological disasters of which ecologists are constantly reminding us. Having thrown off our proper sense of stewardship for this world God has given us, we think we can do what we like with his creation, abusing it in any way with impunity.

Here is the cause of all those failed socialist dreams, of which the collapse of the Communist bloc is the most recent and tragic example. We human beings are just too greedy, too selfish, too lazy, too corrupt to make such utopian dreams of economic cooperation come true. Here is the spark from which the fire of revolutionary violence spreads its cruel terrorism around our world today, the anarchism which is convinced that somehow it's nobler and more dignified to blow up representatives of authority than to submit to them.

Here too is the soil from which the awful spectre of tyranny continues to haunt the human race, armed now with all the weaponry of psychological manipulation and computerized surveillance with which modern science has endowed it. We human beings have a power complex. Like an incompetent actor determined to play Hamlet, so puny man has ambitions to play God. And he is congenitally incapable of realizing that the role is too big for him. So instead of giving power to humble men and women who might lead nations along the path of moderation and peace, again and again we invest power in the megalomaniacs – the Stalins, the Hitlers, the Saddam Husseins – and then winge at the leviathan of control and intimidation with which they encircle us and destroy our freedom.

It all comes down to the same thing. We are not content to be tenants of the vineyard. We insist on being owners. The ingratitude of it is bad enough: that God should bestow such privilege and dignity on the human race, such potential for creative endeavour, and that we should be so little prepared to render anything back to God. But it is the futility of it which is so pathetic. For it's a rebellion doomed to failure. The insane insolence of it, that puny creatures should wave their fists at omnipotence, rejecting anything and everybody that God sends to remind us of the debt that we owe him, and think that we'll get away with it! Surely he won't tolerate it! Will he?

The extraordinary thing about Jesus' story is that he tolerates it for so long.

2. How Jesus understood his own mission

'What shall I do? I will send my son, whom I love; perhaps they will respect him' (Luke 20:13).

I find a pathos in this verse which is intensely moving. Jesus portrays here the patience of God, who has provided rebel human beings with one opportunity after another for repentance, only to find himself slapped in the face every time. Yet still he desires to show his mercy; still he restrains his righteous indignation and turns the other cheek. He will offer one last chance, even if it means gambling with the most precious thing he has: 'My son, whom I love.'

But we must not allow the emotional power of those words to obscure their vital theological significance. I want you to remember again the demand that provoked this parable in the first place. 'Tell us by what authority are you doing these things. Who gave you this authority?' (Luke 20:2).

It's hard to escape the conclusion that here in the story Jesus is giving a straight answer to that question. 'I will send my son, whom I love.' In a remarkable way Jesus has introduced himself as a character in his own story. If we have any doubts, they are surely dispelled by the addition of that qualifying phrase, 'whom I love', because that's the very same word that came from heaven when Jesus was baptized by John back in Luke 3:21–22. 'You are my Son, whom I love,' said the voice from heaven. The coincidence is just too great, especially when you recall that Jesus had just made a direct reference to the baptism of John shortly before.

There is no missing Jesus' implied assertion, then. The prophets who came before were servants of God. 'But I am different,' he says. 'I am special. I am the beloved Son.' I don't believe that the importance of that self-identification by Jesus can be exaggerated.

This is especially so in our day. Let me tell you why. In the last thirty years or so, liberal theology in this country and indeed around the world has been conducting a relentless public campaign to discredit the doctrine of the deity of Christ. The whole idea of God having a Son who comes to earth in the shape of a man, they argue, is a fantastic fairy tale which no modern person can be expected to entertain any longer. John Robinson launched the first public salvo back in 1963 with the notorious *Honest to God*. Then came a Baptist, Michael Taylor, with a similar public statement in 1971. In 1977 we had the Anglican symposium entitled *The Myth of God Incarnate*.

In 1984 one of the contributors, Don Cupitt, pushed the matter even more firmly into the public eye with his TV series *The Sea of Faith*. Most recently, of course, David Jenkins, the former Bishop of Durham, has kept the pot boiling with his newspaper interviews.

The reason for this academic conspiracy is not hard to discern. It is the doctrine of the deity of Christ which more than anything else obstructs dialogue between Christianity and other faiths. And such dialogue comes close to becoming an obsession with many of our contemporary theologians and churchmen. Do you want to be rejected as a candidate for the Christian ministry in any of the mainstream denominations today? Tell the candidates' panel that you want to see Muslims in this country converted to Christ. That's all they need to hear.

If only they can rob Christ of his divinity, so that he becomes one among many servants of God rather than the 'only begotten Son' of the church's Creed, then the way is wide open for major rapprochement between Christianity and Islam, Christianity and Hinduism, Christianity and just about anything else. The ecumenical dream of a single world religion can dawn.

They insist that such a reinterpretation of the person of Christ is possible, even desirable. Why? 'Because,' say these scholars, 'Jesus would never have claimed deity. An alien God-incarnate identity has been superimposed upon Jesus of Nazareth by the Christians who came after him. He would be highly embarrassed to hear us calling him Lord and God.' The deity of Christ, they maintain, is an invention of the early church. It was never part of Jesus' own teaching. So, at least, liberal scholarship asserts.

But that, I suggest to you, is most certainly not the implication of this parable. On the contrary, Jesus here displays a clear sense of his own uniqueness. 'I am the Son', he says, quite distinct from the servants, the prophets who came before.

For the Son bears not just the divine Word, but the

divine likeness. The Son comes not merely to represent the King, but to be the King. Jesus sees himself as no accident of history. He comes with the most specific purpose of asserting the Father's territorial rights over his rebellious vineyard. He comes, in a word, as the Messiah, to inaugurate the long-heralded kingdom of God of which those prophets had spoken.

There's only one way to avoid the conclusion that Jesus entertained such an understanding of himself. That is, to discard this parable as pure invention. And that, of course, is what the scholars do. They can't bear the thought that Jesus would have incorporated himself into a parable in this way as the Son, so they insist that the story has been worked over by later Christians to such an extent that its original form is now totally lost to us. But, frankly, there are no grounds at all for such a dismissal of Luke's record. Only prejudice of a most gross and blinkered kind could persuade anyone to deny that Jesus is here confessing a most remarkable filial consciousness. 'I am the Son,' he says, 'not merely a rabbi, not even a prophet. I am the Son of God and it is by virtue of that divine sonship that I exercise the authority in the temple of which you complain.'

Notice again the wistfulness of that divine soliloquy as the story continues: 'Perhaps they will respect him.' God surely says the same today, as he looks upon the church and upon the world. I know it is irritating to the modern liberal mindset to say that one religion is better than the other. In our pluralist generation all the pressures are upon us to paint Jesus in non-exclusive colours; a prophet, a philosopher, a guru, anything will do.

But flattering though such titles are, there's nothing unique about them. You can admire such people without following them. You can ignore them, if you wish, without cost. But Jesus will not allow us to damn him with faint praise in that way. He claims to be God's last resort, his final Word, his beloved Son.

There will be no dissidents in heaven. There will be nobody saying, 'Three cheers for Muhammad.' If Jesus is right, heaven is united by a single unanimous verdict: 'Jesus is Lord.' And if that's so, we've got to listen to him. We've got to respect his authority. We have no choice.

But the awful truth is, we didn't. And the extraordinary truth is, he knew we wouldn't.

> *But when the tenants saw him, they talked the matter over. 'This is the heir,' they said. 'Let's kill him, and the inheritance will be ours.' So they threw him out of the vineyard and killed him* (Luke 20: 14–15).

There are so many dimensions to the significance of the cross that we couldn't possibly encapsulate its full meaning in a few words. Perhaps that's why we have to make it into a visual symbol. But in this parable, Jesus is focusing down on one element that perhaps we often miss in our theologizing about its significance. The cross, he says, is the ultimate insult. The cross is the supreme gesture of human contempt for the rule of God. The cross is the final snub that puts the lid on centuries of snubs that God has received from the human race. We could not appreciate or even tolerate anyone who challenges us to admit the debt we owe, who calls us to recognize our accountability to our Maker. So we crucified him.

At that point, it's all too easy for you and me once again to shelter behind the fact that Jesus was directly addressing first-century Jews in this parable. 'Oh yes,' we can say. 'It was their fault. The Jews, the Romans, we all know how barbaric they were. The crucifixion was an appalling judicial murder; of course it was. Why, when I watched *Ben Hur* last Christmas, my eyes were wet with tears at the injustice of it all.'

But no, we cannot isolate ourselves from blame in that way. To do so is not to engage with this parable as Jesus wants us to engage with it, but to run away from it. The whole point of what Jesus is saying is that we are tenants too. We were there when they crucified the Lord.

Some of us were with those Roman bureaucrats, some with those violent soldiers. Some of us were among the Pharisees, smug in our biblical orthodoxy. But where were most of us? Statistics dictate that we were in that mindless crowd shouting, 'Crucify him! Crucify him!'

Our hands were not the actual hands that drove the nails through Jesus' hands. But our hearts are wicked, rebellious and irresponsible enough to have done it. I suppose we can plead ignorance. Indeed, Jesus pleaded it for us. 'Father, forgive them,' he said, 'for they do not know what they are doing' (Luke 23:34).

But this parable surely exposes the generosity of that prayer, and the shallowness of such an excuse. For if we crucified him in ignorance, it was nevertheless culpable ignorance. Jesus insists that these tenants knew only too well who it was they were murdering. That's why they were doing it. 'This is the heir,' they said. 'Let's kill him, and the inheritance will be ours.'

So Jesus would have us realize that deep down at the most profound levels of our personal honesty, we too know who he is and we too know why we don't want him in our lives. It is that obsessive desire for independence, that lunatic ambition to play god. 'I don't want any patronizing deity interfering in my life. I want to do my own thing, thank you very much. I want to be my own master. This is the heir; let's kill him and the inheritance will be ours.' We've all said it. And every time we say it we add our personal nail to those that held Christ to his cross.

3. How Jesus understood the future

What then will the owner of the vineyard do to them? (Luke 20:15).

Once again, in its initial reference, this verse predicts the way in which the Jews, by their rejection of the Messiah, forfeited their spiritual privileges to the Gentiles. Matthew puts it clearly in his vision of this parable. 'The kingdom of God will be taken away from you', he says, 'and given to a people who will produce its fruit' (Matthew 21:43). It's understandable that the Jewish audience were offended, for such a prospect tore the stuffing out of all those messianic dreams of theirs. As patriots, they were looking forward to the kingdom of God. It would be a day of triumph for the Jewish nation. 'No,' says Jesus, 'not at all. The kingdom of God spells a day of national catastrophe for the Jewish nation.'

But just as it would be foolish of us to think that the only wicked tenants in this world are Jews, so it would be an even greater folly to assume that they are the only people God is angry with in this world. No, it is with the solemn prospect of judgment to come that Jesus confronts *all* of us at the end of his story.

He confronts the visible church with that prospect, for if the leaders of Jerusalem forfeited the spiritual privilege of Israel to the Gentiles because they failed to honour and respect God's Son as they should, what will God do to those so-called theologians and clerics who in their zeal for interfaith dialogue deny the uniqueness of Christ? Is it any surprise that the mainstream denominations of our nation are declining in membership and influence today? Is it any surprise that new Christian groups who are not embarrassed to own a divine Christ as their Lord are capturing the initiative in our land today?

The Archbishop of Canterbury, George Carey, is right when he talks of the next few years as critical for the Church of England. There are clear signs that God is giving the vineyard to others under the very noses of the bishops. I'm just hoping that George Carey is courageous enough and honest enough to admit that it is the defection from the apostolic faith of the New Testament on the part of some of those bishops which is largely responsible. The glory is departing from some of our mainstream denominations, because of undisciplined error in the most fundamental matter of the lordship of Christ.

Jesus confronts the nation of Britain, too, with this prospect of final judgment. For if Israel had known blessing from God's help over the centuries, so has this land of ours. For a thousand years Christianity has been the official faith of this land. We were delivered from paganism in the distant past, from Islam in the Middle Ages, from apostate Catholicism in the sixteenth century, and from Fascist and Marxist dictatorship in this twentieth century. God has spared this country politically in most remarkable ways, time and time again.

More than that, he has blessed this nation with preachers of extraordinary power and influence: godly men who have called us as a nation to place ourselves under the authority of God; martyrs who have died to bring us the Bible; evangelists who have spent their lives promoting revival. There are churches and chapels in every town and village testifying to God's signal goodness to this land.

What then will God do to us if, in the face of all that blessing, this land today turns its back on its Christian heritage and embraces a secularism as godless in its immorality and pagan in its superstition as many nations that have enjoyed not a fraction of its privileges?

Is it any wonder that economic prosperity is drying up, that the crime rate soars, that our international influence declines? Our world is littered with wrecks of great empires and nations of the past. There is nothing immortal about Great Britain.

But perhaps supremely we have to face the fact that Jesus confronts each of us as individuals with the prospect of final judgment, in these sobering and solemn words at the end of his story.

To us, Jesus' comments after the story, in verses 17–18, may seem difficult. But to Luke's readers they made eminent sense. For Jesus is fusing together here three verses with which they were very familiar. The New Testament quotes them often. Perhaps they come to Jesus' mind here because they are all about stones. And in the Aramaic language that he spoke, the word for 'stone' and the word for 'son' sound almost identical.

The first quotation is from Psalm 118, and speaks metaphorically of the construction of a house. The masons building the house discover an oddly shaped stone that won't fit in the wall. At first they discard it, but then when they get to the very top of the building they realize that this is just the piece of rock they need to complete the supporting arch, the brick without which the whole edifice would otherwise collapse – the chief cornerstone.

In its original setting this psalm applied the metaphor to the king of Israel on his return to Jerusalem after a successful military campaign. The pagan nations had treated the king of Israel with contempt, and they discarded him like a worthless pebble. But now God has vindicated his anointed one and exalted him over his enemies. So the stone the builders had rejected has become the capstone. 'It's the Lord's doing and it's marvellous in our eyes,' they sang.

But to the Jews of Jesus' day this entire psalm was interpreted messianically. Indeed, we encounter a chorus of it on the lips of the crowd as they welcome Jesus triumphantly into Jerusalem on Palm Sunday: 'Blessed is the king who comes in the name of the Lord' (Luke 19:38).

So Jesus is pointing out the full implications of Psalm 118 to these so-called Bible students who were challenging him. 'If, as you believe, this is a messianic prophecy, then don't you see what it implies? It implies that the powerful men of this world will repudiate the Messiah just as those pagan nations repudiated the king of Israel of old. But then God will lift him to his rightful place of exaltation. My story of the rejected son is confirmed in that scripture you know so well, the scripture of the rejected stone.'

And before they can recover from this startling expository insight, with a stroke of genius Jesus welds on two more verses from Isaiah 8 and Daniel 2 which also speak about stones. The Isaiah text cautions that if Israel does not trust the Lord, then the Lord himself will become like a stone over which they stumble. The quotation from Daniel speaks of a stone or a rock symbolizing the kingdom of God, which will be used at the end of the age as a hammer in God's hands to destroy all the opposing kingdoms of the earth and smash them to smithereens.

And by fusing all these scriptures together, Jesus is issuing a solemn warning. The stone the builders discarded, he says, now lies on the ground. You are plotting to murder God's Son. Careless people stumble over him to their destruction, as Isaiah said they would. But one day soon he will be raised up to the top of the arch. And for people who are foolish enough still to reject him then, it will no longer be they who fall over him, but rather he who falls on them, as Daniel predicted. 'It is a dangerous thing', he says, 'to reject me. You are playing with fire. Put yourself in the owner's place in my story and you will realize why. Do you really think God is going to tolerate the preposterous insolence of the human race for ever? Do you think he will stand idly by and grant his beloved Son no vindication in the face of his enemies?'

No, a day of accounting is coming. 'What you do with me,' he says, 'the Son, the Stone, will determine your final destiny on that day. You must choose either to be broken voluntarily by me, your rebellious pride humbled and chastened by recognition of who I am; or you must choose to be finally crushed by me, judged, condemned for your complicity in this rebel world.' This is a solemn message. But I fear it's one that, as churches and preachers, we are growing reluctant to be frank about.

It's a great mistake to confuse divine patience with divine indifference. According to this story, God is being patient with us human beings, sending one servant after another and finally sending his own Son. The danger is, we could be deceived into thinking that his patience is infinite. But Jesus says it is not. The heart of God is unbearably provoked. You must not mistake his patience for indifference.

It's popular to speak of God as a kindly old fellow, all love, who would never harm a fly. But where have we got the idea from? It certainly wasn't from Jesus. It is God's moral indignation against evil that prevents his love from degenerating into mere sentimentality. We don't really admire people who are never angry. There are times when righteousness demands anger – at cruelty, at prejudice, for example. We can't respect a person who remains in some kind of insulated benignity when confronted by real wickedness.

If there are times when people ought to be angry, how much more, then, will there be a time when God will be angry! Do not mistake patience for indifference. He's patient with us men and women, but not indifferent towards our sins. We are accountable; and ultimately we shall give account of that missing rent, account for those injured servants, account for that murdered Son.

How does Jesus see the future? He sees it as a day of accounting, a day of judgment. Samuel Johnson remarked, 'I remember that my Maker has said that he will place the sheep on his right hand and the goats on his left. That is a solemn truth which this frivolous age needs to hear.' The frivolous age he was talking about was the eighteenth century, but there's plenty of frivolity still around.

It disturbs me most profoundly that so few people today take hell seriously. Many of those theologians I mentioned earlier are universalists, insisting that hell is a sub-Christian superstition. 'Who can possibly imagine a loving God tolerating such an obscenity?'

More popularly, people joke about it. 'Well, if I go to hell there'll be plenty of people who'll go with me' – as if hell were going to be some jolly party for the society of the free spirits. I do not deny that the language of judgment the Bible sometimes uses is difficult. I sympathize with some who find the doctrine of hell confusing and unpalatable. I would agree that Jesus uses symbolical language when he speaks of 'hell fire'. But I cannot believe he would use such language unless he wanted to warn us of something real and dreadful. And I cannot believe that the Son of God would have hung on the cross amid such agony if he did not want to spare us something even worse. Of course judgment is real. It's because judgment is real that we need rescue. The very word 'salvation' would be meaningless if there was nothing to be saved from.

Here is a God, I say, who sees us as individuals walking into misery, determined to be what by very nature we cannot be; independent of him. He puts up signposts in our path to warn us; he sends messengers to try and persuade us; but we despise and ignore them. He even sends his own Son, and he watches as we murder him. Yet still he persists in urging us to come to our senses. Still he persists in urging us to discover our true human destiny in fellowship with him as tenants of his world, not as usurpers of it.

But if we insist upon our autonomy, he will give it to us. In that sense he doesn't have to send any of us to hell. Our tragedy is that we are already walking there. The one principle of hell is, 'I am on my own.' If we tell God to leave us alone, Jesus says, then at the end of the day that's just what he will do: leave us alone permanently. The Bible says it is a fearful thing to fall into the hands of the living God, but I'll tell you something that scares me even more. And that's falling out of his hands.

> '*What then will the owner of the vineyard do to them? He will come and kill those tenants and give the vineyard to others.*'
>
> *When the people heard this, they said, 'May this never be!*' (Luke 20:15–16).

Should not those words generate a great concern for holiness in us? Should they not generate a great passion for evangelism in us? Should they not generate in us a great seriousness about this Christian faith? If we are backsliding from a faith in Christ we once professed, or if we are uncommitted to Christ altogether, should those words not generate in us a great concern for our eternal destiny? What will he do with you?

Do you notice that phrase with which Luke introduces the finale to Jesus' story? 'Jesus looked directly at them,' it says. There's a strange intensity about that, isn't there? He fixed his eyes upon these people. What was in that look as he issued this solemn final warning to them? Urgency, pity, appeal, love? Yes, love surely more than anything. For these were the eyes which, just a few hours before, had been weeping for Jerusalem.

Can we not then sense that Christ looks directly at us? He looks at us with that same intensity, that same urgency. All the love of God for us stupid, sinful, wayward men and women is concentrated in that gaze. For we were there, with all the other rebellious tenants; we were there when they crucified the Lord.

We have insulted God. We have presumed upon his patience too long. We have despised his generosity too long. We have treated his Son as a second-class feature in our lives too long. He waits now, patiently, but not indifferently, for our apology, and for the payment of that long-overdue debt of moral obedience we owe him. He is not going to wait for ever.